Beyond the Drink: Stories of Struggle, Growth, and Redemption

David M.

Published by David M., 2024.

While every precaution has been taken in the preparation of this book, the publisher assumes no responsibility for errors or omissions, or for damages resulting from the use of the information contained herein.

BEYOND THE DRINK: STORIES OF STRUGGLE, GROWTH, AND REDEMPTION

First edition. October 22, 2024.

Copyright © 2024 David M..

ISBN: 979-8227355744

Written by David M..

For those who have faced the shadows of addiction and emerged into the light of recovery. May your journeys inspire hope and resilience in others. This book is dedicated to the friends, families, and communities that support us on our paths to healing—thank you for believing in the possibility of change.

Preface to Beyond the Drink: Stories of Struggle, Growth, and Redemption

In every corner of the world, alcohol occupies a complex and multifaceted role in our lives. For many, it serves as a source of joy and connection—a way to celebrate milestones, forge friendships, and create cherished memories. Yet for others, it can transform into a shadowy figure, leading to struggles, isolation, and despair. As a recovering alcoholic myself, I have experienced this duality firsthand, and it is this very complexity that I aim to explore in *Beyond the Drink*.

This collection of stories delves into the profound impact of alcohol on individuals and the cultures they inhabit. Each narrative reflects the unique experiences of those navigating their relationships with drinking, capturing the essence of human struggle and the possibility of redemption. From the revelry of a bustling British pub to the intimate reflections of women grappling with addiction, these tales reveal the rich tapestry of life intertwined with alcohol.

While my journey has been fraught with challenges, it has also been paved with moments of clarity, connection, and newfound purpose. Each character in this collection represents a facet of the human experience—reminding us that we are never truly alone in our struggles. Their stories showcase the courage it takes to confront one's demons and the strength found in vulnerability.

In *Beyond the Drink*, we journey through various perspectives. We meet Dr. Bob, who navigates the complexities of addiction within the medical community; we explore heartfelt struggles faced by women in their battles with alcohol; and we witness the cultural influences of drinking across Europe as the protagonist seeks to understand their place within these traditions. Each story weaves together themes of struggle, growth, and redemption, illustrating the transformative power of confronting our past and embracing a future free from the weight of addiction.

As you read these stories, I invite you to reflect on your own relationship with alcohol and the impact it has had on your life and those around you. My hope is that these narratives inspire compassion, understanding, and a deeper awareness of the complexities of drinking culture.

Ultimately, *Beyond the Drink* is a testament to the resilience of the human spirit. It serves as a reminder that even in our darkest moments, there is hope for healing and connection. Together, let us raise a glass to the stories of struggle and redemption, celebrating the journey toward a more mindful and meaningful existence—beyond the drink.

Thank you for joining me on this journey. Cheers to new beginnings.

A Doctor's Descent: The Horrors of Addiction

Prologue: The Bottomless Pit

Dr. Andrew B. had always been admired. Tall and composed, with a sharp mind and steady hands, he was the man people trusted in their most vulnerable moments. The type of doctor who could perform surgery with precision, reassuring families with a calm confidence that all would be well. His patients saw him as a pillar of strength, and his colleagues respected him for his dedication and intellect. In the hospital halls, he was the doctor others aspired to be—a picture of success.

But beneath that polished exterior lay a man drowning in his own secrets. Alcohol had become his constant companion, the quiet refuge he sought after long days in the operating room. At first, it was a glass of whiskey to take the edge off the day, a simple indulgence. Then it became two. And then more. What began as a way to relax slowly turned into a crutch, and that crutch had become a prison. Dr. B.'s life had split in two—on the surface, he was the respected surgeon, but inside, his world was crumbling.

At home, his wife had grown distant, tired of making excuses for his absences, tired of seeing the empty bottles in his study. His children barely saw him anymore, and when they did, his once-loving embrace was often replaced by slurred words and the smell of alcohol. He told himself he was in control, that no one noticed, but he was wrong. His performance in the operating room had started to slip. His once-flawless surgeries were now marred by mistakes, small at first but growing more dangerous with each passing week.

The night it all fell apart was supposed to be routine—a simple appendectomy, a surgery he had performed countless times. But Andrew was not sober that evening. The drinks he had during lunch were supposed to be the last for the day, but they hadn't been. His hands, usually steady as a rock, were shaky. His vision blurred under the harsh lights of the operating room. And then it happened—the scalpel slipped, a single moment of hesitation leading to a mistake that would change everything. The patient, a young girl, went into cardiac arrest. The team worked frantically to save her, but the damage had been done.

In the aftermath, Andrew stood numbly as the family was informed of their daughter's condition. His mind raced, panic swelling in his chest, but outwardly, he remained calm, playing the role of the concerned doctor. But inside, he knew. He knew the truth he could never admit—that his drinking had caused this.

That night, alone in his office, he stared at the whiskey bottle on his desk. For a moment, he considered calling his wife, telling her everything, begging for help. But instead, he poured another glass, the amber liquid swirling as he raised it to his lips. The familiar warmth washed over him, momentarily numbing the guilt and the fear.

But as the warmth faded, the pit remained. Deeper, darker, and more suffocating than ever before. Dr. Andrew B., once a man of skill and success, was falling, spiraling into a bottomless pit from which he could see no escape. Little did he know, this was the moment that would lead him to the most important journey of his life—the fight for his own redemption.

Part I: Descent into Darkness

Chapter 1: The Promising Beginning

Andrew B.'s fascination with medicine began in childhood. Growing up in a small town, he was known for his curiosity about how things worked. While other kids played with toys, Andrew spent hours reading books about the human body and pestering the town doctor with questions. His passion was undeniable. He wanted to be more than just an observer of life—he wanted to fix what was broken, to heal people. That ambition drove him through school, earning him top grades and, ultimately, a coveted spot in one of the country's most prestigious medical schools.

Medical school was grueling, but Andrew thrived under the pressure. The late nights spent studying, the endless rounds of clinicals, the stress of being in life-or-death situations—it was all fuel for his growing determination to be the best. He developed a reputation among his peers and professors for his skill, work ethic, and calm demeanor under pressure. Even the most seasoned surgeons took note of his surgical precision, predicting he'd rise quickly in the ranks.

As he transitioned from student to resident, his dedication never wavered. Andrew was known for his ability to take on the toughest cases, often working back-to-back shifts without a word of complaint. His mentors saw in him the qualities of a great surgeon: confidence, intellect, and focus. It wasn't long before he landed a coveted position in a prestigious hospital, his career on a fast track to success.

He married young, to a woman named Emily who had supported him through the chaos of medical school. They were the picture-perfect couple—both driven and successful, with a shared dream of building a life together. Andrew's future seemed bright. His name was being whispered in hospital circles, and his work was catching the eye of prominent medical boards. He was well on his way to becoming one of the top surgeons in the country.

But alongside his growing professional success came a slow but steady shift in his personal life. The pressure, while thrilling at first, began to weigh on him in ways he hadn't anticipated. The long hours, the constant stress of life-or-death decisions, and the feeling that he could never make a mistake began to creep into his mind. At the end of a long day, Andrew found that a glass of wine or whiskey helped him unwind. It was harmless, he told himself—everyone needed a way to relax.

At first, it was just at social gatherings or during dinner with colleagues. A glass of wine, a toast to a successful surgery, a bit of whiskey after a particularly long day. His drinking seemed normal, even sophisticated. It helped him loosen up, and he was still performing at the top of his game, so no one questioned it—not even himself.

As time passed, however, the social drinking began to bleed into his everyday routine. He started having a drink after every shift, not just the tough ones. It became a small reward after a long surgery or a stressful meeting. A glass to relax before bed turned into two, then three. His wife Emily noticed, but Andrew brushed off her concerns. After all, he was a surgeon, he reasoned—a man in control of his life, his career, his decisions. He was succeeding in every way that mattered, so what harm could a drink or two possibly do?

What Andrew didn't realize was that the seeds of addiction were already taking root. The very thing that helped him manage his stress was slowly gaining control over him. The high of success was being replaced by a need to numb the growing pressure. And though Andrew couldn't see it yet, his promising beginning was leading him down a path he wouldn't be able to control for much longer. The once-driven doctor was on the verge of a descent into darkness, and his journey was only beginning.

Chapter 2: The Hidden Disease

The change was gradual, so slow that even Andrew didn't notice it at first. What began as an occasional drink to take the edge off after a stressful shift started to feel less like a choice and more like a necessity. The whiskey glass he kept on his study desk became a nightly fixture, then an early-morning one on the weekends, and eventually, it was there during his lunch breaks. The drinking was no longer just about unwinding—it was about escaping. The pressure of his growing reputation, the constant demand for perfection, and the weight of decisions that could mean life or death—it all became too much. Alcohol dulled the intensity of it all, if only for a little while.

As Andrew's reliance on alcohol grew, so did his ability to hide it. At work, he maintained the same composed, confident exterior. His surgeries were still mostly flawless, and he continued to receive praise from his colleagues and superiors. He wore the mask of a man in control, but behind closed doors, things were beginning to unravel. His once-loving marriage with Emily had turned cold. She had stopped mentioning his drinking outright, but the tension between them was palpable. The late-night arguments over his erratic behavior had faded into a silent distance, the kind that grows slowly and corrodes the foundation of a relationship. Emily wasn't blind to his drinking; she saw the empty bottles piling up, noticed the slurred speech when he came home late, and the glazed look in his eyes when they were supposed to be having dinner. But every time she brought it up, Andrew brushed it off.

"I'm fine, Emily. It's just stress from work," he'd say. "I've got it under control."

But control was slipping further from his grasp each day.

His ability to hide his drinking extended into the hospital as well. Andrew had learned to manage the symptoms of his growing addiction—he knew how to time his drinks so he wasn't visibly intoxicated during rounds or surgeries. He would chew mints to mask the smell of alcohol on his breath, and he became adept at avoiding situations where someone might notice the subtle tremors in his hands. The very same hands that had once been celebrated for their steady precision were now starting to shake from withdrawal if he went too long without a drink.

Still, Andrew convinced himself that he was functioning. He hadn't lost a patient yet, after all. He was still able to perform complex surgeries, give presentations, and even attend charity galas with Emily by his side. No one outside of his home had any reason to suspect the truth, and even Emily's concerns seemed more like an annoyance than a real threat. He told himself that successful men drank to manage stress—that alcohol was part of the deal when you worked in such a high-pressure field.

But his body told a different story. His hangovers became more brutal, his concentration slipping during even the most routine tasks. His tolerance for alcohol skyrocketed, requiring more and more to achieve the same effect. There were moments in surgery where he would blink too long, losing focus for just a second, his mind swimming in the fog of the previous night's drinking. Those brief moments of confusion terrified him, but he pushed the fear aside, drowning it with another drink once the surgery was over.

At home, his relationship with Emily continued to deteriorate. Where there had once been love and laughter, now there was resentment and silence. She no longer waited up for him, choosing instead to go to bed early, her back turned to him when he finally stumbled in late at night. Their children, once close to their father, now barely saw him. He missed school events and family dinners more often than not, always using work as an excuse, though in truth, he had started staying out later to drink without judgment.

There were nights when Andrew would come home and barely remember how he got there, collapsing into bed in a haze of alcohol and regret. He knew, somewhere deep inside, that he was losing control. His drinking was no longer just a way to relax—it had become his solution to everything: stress, failure, loneliness. But the more he drank, the more problems seemed to arise. Patients started to notice his distracted behavior, and a few whispered that Dr. B. wasn't as sharp as he used to be. Nurses gave him concerned looks when he showed up late for rounds, his eyes bloodshot and his hands trembling ever so slightly.

The first time he completely lost track of a conversation during surgery, he panicked internally. He had been standing over the operating table, scalpel in hand, and for a brief moment, he couldn't remember what he was supposed to do next. His mind went blank, the world around him fading into a blur. He managed to cover it up, moving forward with the procedure, but his heart raced, his body flooded with fear. He needed to stop, he told himself. He needed to cut back, get things under control again. But instead of stopping, he drank even more that night, trying to erase the memory of his failure.

As time went on, Andrew's performance continued to slip. He made more small mistakes, ones that were easy enough to explain away but were beginning to pile up. His colleagues noticed, and so did Emily. But Andrew remained in denial, clinging to the belief that he could still function, that he was still in control.

What he didn't realize was that the disease of alcoholism had already taken hold of him. It was no longer a choice; it was a compulsion, a need that consumed him more with each passing day. His life, once so full of promise, was beginning to collapse around him, and yet he couldn't stop. Not yet. Not until the bottom dropped out completely.

Chapter 3: The Walls Close In

Andrew B. stood in front of the mirror, staring at a man he no longer recognized. His once vibrant eyes were now dull and bloodshot, and the sharp features that had defined his face were softened by exhaustion and neglect. Dark circles formed beneath his eyes, telling the story of sleepless nights and the relentless hangovers that followed his daily drinking. His reflection seemed like a ghost, a hollow version of the man who had once been so full of life and ambition.

He splashed cold water on his face, trying to shake off the grogginess that hung over him like a dark cloud. He had a surgery in an hour, but his hands were trembling, his stomach in knots. His morning routine had changed drastically—no longer just a cup of coffee to start the day, but now a shot of whiskey, hidden in his travel mug. It calmed the shakes, or so he convinced himself. But deep down, he knew something had shifted. The alcohol was no longer just a crutch; it had become a trap, one he could not escape.

As the weeks turned into months, Andrew's behavior became more erratic. The drinking was no longer contained to the evenings or weekends. Now, it seeped into every part of his day. A flask hidden in his desk drawer, another bottle tucked away in his car for emergencies. He drank before surgeries, after surgeries, and in between rounds. His colleagues had begun to notice. Nurses whispered behind his back, concerned about his increasingly disheveled appearance and slurred speech during consultations. He was late more often, missing meetings or showing up unprepared.

One morning, he arrived late to a high-profile surgery—a procedure that had been scheduled for weeks, with a renowned visiting surgeon in attendance. Andrew stumbled into the operating room, his face flushed, his breath carrying the faint scent of alcohol. He tried to focus, to clear his mind, but the room seemed to sway beneath him. Halfway through the operation, he made a mistake. A small slip of the scalpel, a cut too deep. The visiting surgeon had to step in, taking over to save the patient from further harm. Andrew stood there, frozen, the weight of his failure crashing down on him.

Later, in the hospital hallway, the visiting surgeon confronted him. "What the hell happened in there, B.?" he asked, his voice low but stern. Andrew mumbled an excuse about being tired, about overworking himself. But the visiting surgeon saw through it, shaking his head in disappointment. "Get it together, or you'll kill someone."

The shame was unbearable. He went home that night and drank until he blacked out, desperate to drown the voice in his head that screamed of failure.

At home, his marriage had all but disintegrated. Emily, once his partner and confidante, barely spoke to him anymore. The distance between them had grown into a chasm. She had tried, in the beginning, to understand, to be patient. But now, she couldn't even look at him without a mixture of anger and sadness in her eyes. Their children had learned to tiptoe around him, sensing the tension in the house, avoiding him whenever he came home late. The laughter that once filled their home had been replaced with silence, and the warmth of family dinners had long since faded.

Emily had given him an ultimatum one night, her voice trembling with frustration. "I can't do this anymore, Andrew. You need to get help, or I'm taking the kids and leaving."

He had promised her—just as he had promised himself—that he would cut back, that he would stop. But the next morning, the bottle called to him again, and his promises dissolved in the amber liquid. He was trapped in a vicious cycle of self-loathing and alcohol, each drink deepening the pit he had fallen into. No matter how much he wanted to stop, he couldn't. The compulsion to drink had overtaken his willpower, and the shame of his failures only drove him further into the bottle.

At work, things were spiraling out of control. His once impeccable reputation was tarnished. Patients began requesting other doctors, fearful of his distracted demeanor and late arrivals. The hospital board had taken notice, too. Rumors were circulating that Dr. B. wasn't the surgeon he once was, that something was off. A formal complaint had been filed after the incident in the operating room with the visiting surgeon. He was called in for a meeting with the hospital administrator, where they gently suggested that he take a leave of absence. It was framed as concern for his well-being, but Andrew knew what it really meant: they didn't trust him anymore.

Physically, his body was beginning to break down. The headaches were constant, and his hands shook so badly some mornings that he could barely hold a coffee cup. His skin was pallid, and his weight fluctuated as his appetite disappeared. Every time he looked in the mirror, the reflection showed a man who was wasting away, consumed by a disease he couldn't name. He had always been in control—of his life, his career, his family. But now, alcohol had taken that control from him. And no matter how much he tried to fight it, he was losing.

There were moments—brief, fleeting moments—where Andrew felt a surge of panic and desperation. He would sit in his office, the weight of the flask in his hand, and feel the crushing reality of his situation. He was a doctor, a man who saved lives, yet he couldn't save his own. The guilt gnawed at him, the shame of what he had become. He was no longer the promising surgeon, the loving husband, the devoted father. He was an alcoholic, trapped in a disease that was destroying everything he had worked for.

In those moments of despair, he considered reaching out for help. But the thought of admitting his weakness, of showing the world that he wasn't the man they thought he was, terrified him. So instead, he took another drink, and the walls closed in tighter around him.

The man who had once held the power to heal was now powerless to save himself. And the realization that he was trapped—that no matter how much he hated himself for it, he couldn't stop drinking—filled him with a despair so deep it seemed there was no way out.

Part II: Hitting Rock Bottom

Chapter 4: A Life Unraveled

The day that shattered Andrew B.'s life began like so many others—with a drink. He had woken up nauseous, his hands trembling from withdrawal. The whiskey bottle, half-empty on his bedside table, beckoned. He had promised himself the night before that he would stop. He was going to get clean, turn his life around, and repair the damage he had done. But the promises always felt so far away in the cold light of morning, and as his body screamed for relief, he poured himself a drink and told himself it would be the last.

It was a lie he had told himself countless times.

By the time he arrived at the hospital, the alcohol had dulled the edges of his anxiety, but the fog still hung over him. He had a surgery scheduled that morning—a routine gallbladder removal. He had done it hundreds of times, a procedure as familiar to him as the back of his hand. But as he stood in the operating room, his vision blurred, and the sounds around him seemed distant. He knew something was wrong. His body was weak, his mind unfocused.

Midway through the surgery, disaster struck. His hands slipped at a critical moment, and before he could correct himself, he severed an artery. Blood poured from the incision, and panic gripped the room. The nurses and anesthesiologist sprang into action, but Andrew froze. For a moment, he couldn't move, his mind clouded with fear and alcohol-induced fog. His surgical team tried to control the bleeding, but the damage had been done.

The patient—a man in his forties—died on the table.

The hospital launched an immediate investigation. The loss of the patient was a devastating blow, not just to the man's family, but to Andrew's entire career. He had faced close calls before, but never had he lost a life so directly due to his own actions. Word spread quickly through the hospital. Colleagues whispered in the hallways, nurses gave him pitiful looks, and Andrew knew what they were all thinking: *He wasn't fit to be in that operating room.* The surgeon they once admired had become a liability.

A week later, the hospital board convened to discuss Andrew's future. The review was brutal. His drinking had been suspected for some time, but now there was evidence—his erratic behavior, his frequent absences, and now, a life lost because of his negligence. They suspended him indefinitely, pending further investigation, and ordered him to seek professional help for his drinking. His medical license was on the line.

The news hit Andrew like a wrecking ball. His career, his identity, his entire life had revolved around being a surgeon. Without it, he didn't know who he was. He tried to quit drinking cold turkey that week, but the withdrawals were unbearable. He shook violently, broke into cold sweats, and couldn't keep food down. Desperation clawed at him, but so did the craving for alcohol. After three days of pure agony, he gave in. The relief from the drink was immediate, but so was the crushing guilt that followed.

Emily had had enough. When she found him drunk in the middle of the day, slumped on the living room couch, she packed her bags. She had been threatening to leave for months, but this time was different. She took the kids and walked out the door without another word. Andrew begged her to stay, tears streaming down his face, but she was resolute. He had broken too many promises, told too many lies. As she drove away, Andrew collapsed on the front steps, utterly alone.

The days blurred together after that. His once orderly life was now in complete disarray. The hospital's suspension meant no income, and without Emily's salary, bills began to pile up. The mortgage went unpaid, collection notices arrived in the mail, and Andrew began to lose what little he had left. He stopped answering his phone, avoiding calls from concerned friends and colleagues. Even his closest friends—the few who hadn't already distanced themselves—had begun to withdraw, unsure of how to help a man who couldn't help himself.

Physically, Andrew's health continued to deteriorate. His drinking had escalated to dangerous levels. His liver was failing, his body riddled with signs of alcohol-induced damage. His doctor—ironically, one of his former colleagues—had warned him that if he didn't stop drinking, he wouldn't live to see the next year. But the warning fell on deaf ears. Andrew knew he was dying, but in his mind, that was preferable to facing the reality of his life.

Every night, he would sit in the dark, nursing a bottle of whiskey, replaying the events of the surgery in his mind. The patient's death haunted him. He saw the man's face every time he closed his eyes, heard the cries of the man's family when they were told their loved one hadn't survived. The guilt was unbearable, suffocating. It was as though a heavy weight had settled on his chest, and no matter how much he drank, it wouldn't go away.

He tried to stop again. He tried rehab, attending a treatment center for a few weeks. But it didn't stick. The moment he was back in the real world, the cravings returned, stronger than ever. He was a prisoner in his own body, shackled by an addiction he couldn't break free from. The despair that followed his failed attempts at sobriety only fueled his drinking further. He felt cursed—unable to live with alcohol, but unable to live without it.

As the months passed, the walls of Andrew's world closed in tighter and tighter. The house was falling apart around him, both literally and figuratively. With no money to keep up with repairs, the once beautiful home was now in disrepair, the lawn overgrown, the roof leaking. Inside, it was worse. Empty bottles littered the floors, the smell of stale alcohol permeated the air, and Andrew moved through the days in a haze, barely functioning.

Every now and then, a friend or family member would reach out, offering help, but Andrew pushed them all away. He was too far gone, too ashamed to face anyone. He had lost everything—his career, his family, his health, and his dignity. The man who had once been revered as a brilliant surgeon was now a shadow of himself, broken by the very disease he had spent years denying.

And yet, somewhere deep within him, a tiny flicker of hope remained. He didn't know how to fix his life or whether it could even be fixed. But as he sat there in the wreckage of his world, with nothing left to lose, he knew one thing for certain: if he didn't find a way out of this bottomless pit, he would soon be dead. And for the first time in a long time, Andrew wasn't sure he wanted that.

The road to rock bottom was long and brutal, but now, as the walls finally closed in, Andrew was faced with a choice: continue down this path to certain death, or fight for his life—if he had anything left to fight for.

Chapter 5: The Moment of Clarity

Andrew B. had lost track of time. Days bled into nights, and the cycle of drinking seemed endless. The alcohol numbed the pain, dulled the sharp edges of his shame, but it was never enough. There was always a deeper hole to fall into, and Andrew had been falling for what felt like an eternity.

One cold evening, after a particularly brutal bender, Andrew woke up on the bathroom floor. He didn't remember how he got there, but the sharp pain in his abdomen told him something was very wrong. His body was breaking down, the years of heavy drinking finally catching up to him. He tried to stand, but his legs buckled under him, sending him crashing back to the tile floor. The pain in his stomach intensified, a deep, searing ache that shot through his entire body. He curled up on the floor, clutching his side, his breath coming in shallow gasps.

Hours passed, and the pain didn't subside. His vision blurred, and a cold sweat broke out across his skin. Andrew knew he needed help, but the thought of reaching out to anyone filled him with dread. Who would come? Emily had left him. His friends had all but disappeared. He was alone in a house that reeked of decay, the floor beneath him sticky with spilled whiskey.

But as the pain in his abdomen worsened, Andrew realized he didn't have a choice. His body was shutting down, and if he didn't do something soon, he would die there, on the bathroom floor, a victim of his own destruction. His shaking hand reached for his phone, and with trembling fingers, he dialed 911.

The ambulance arrived within minutes, but it felt like hours. The paramedics lifted him onto the stretcher, and as they carried him out of the house, Andrew caught a glimpse of his reflection in the hallway mirror. The man staring back at him was gaunt, hollow-eyed, a shadow of the once proud surgeon. In that moment, Andrew felt a surge of panic. He wasn't ready to die. Despite everything—the failures, the losses, the pain—there was still a part of him that wanted to live.

At the hospital, the doctors confirmed his worst fear. His liver was failing. Years of heavy drinking had taken a toll, and now his body was paying the price. They stabilized him, but the prognosis was grim. If he didn't stop drinking, his liver would shut down completely, and the damage would be irreversible.

Lying in the hospital bed, connected to IVs and machines that beeped with alarming regularity, Andrew stared at the ceiling, grappling with the truth he had avoided for so long. He was powerless over alcohol. It had consumed his life, taken everything from him, and now it was killing him. He had always believed he was in control, that he could stop whenever he wanted. But now, with death staring him in the face, he realized how wrong he had been.

It wasn't just his body that was broken; it was his spirit. For the first time, he felt the weight of his powerlessness. He couldn't fix this. He couldn't heal himself, no matter how much he wanted to. The realization washed over him like a cold wave—he needed help. Real help. He couldn't do this alone.

In the days that followed, a visitor arrived. It was John, an old colleague from the hospital, someone Andrew hadn't seen in years. John had once been in a similar place, a doctor who had spiraled into alcoholism but had managed to pull himself out. He had heard about Andrew's situation and came to see if there was anything he could do.

John sat down beside Andrew's hospital bed, a kind but serious look in his eyes. "I've been where you are," he said quietly. "I know what it feels like to think there's no way out."

Andrew's pride wanted to push John away, to insist that he didn't need help, that he could manage on his own. But deep down, he knew that wasn't true. So he listened.

John told him about his own battle with alcohol—how he had lost everything, just like Andrew, and how it wasn't until he hit rock bottom that he realized he needed to surrender. "It wasn't about fighting the addiction," John said, his voice steady. "It was about letting go. Admitting that I was powerless and that I couldn't do it alone."

Andrew didn't say much, but something about John's words resonated with him. He had spent so long trying to fight, trying to control everything in his life. But the more he tried to hold on, the more he lost. Maybe the key wasn't in controlling the addiction but in surrendering to something bigger than himself.

John continued, sharing how he had found recovery through a program that focused on spiritual principles. "It's not about religion," he clarified. "It's about finding a higher power, something greater than yourself to lean on. For me, it was God. But for you, it could be anything. The point is, you can't do this on your own."

As John spoke, Andrew felt a shift inside him. The weight of his pride and denial began to lift, replaced by a strange sense of peace. He had never considered himself a spiritual person, but in that moment, he understood what John was saying. His life had been a constant battle for control, and in the end, he had lost that battle. But maybe, just maybe, there was another way forward—one that didn't require him to do it all on his own.

Before John left, he handed Andrew a small, worn book. "Take a look at this when you're ready," he said. "It helped me find a way out, and maybe it can help you too."

Andrew took the book, feeling its weight in his hand. As John walked out of the room, Andrew looked down at the cover. It was a copy of the *Big Book* of Alcoholics Anonymous. He had heard of it before, of course, but he had never imagined he would need it. Yet here he was, at the lowest point of his life, holding onto what might be his last chance for redemption.

That night, as the hospital ward quieted and the lights dimmed, Andrew opened the book and began to read. The words on the page spoke to him in a way he hadn't expected. They told stories of people just like him—people who had lost everything to alcohol, who had felt the same despair, the same hopelessness. And yet, these people had found a way out. They had found recovery through surrender, through admitting their powerlessness and turning to a higher power.

For the first time, Andrew allowed himself to believe that maybe, just maybe, he could find that too.

As he drifted off to sleep, the weight of his guilt and shame still lingered, but there was something else now—a small glimmer of hope. It wasn't much, but it was enough to hold onto. Enough to take the first step toward a different future.

The journey would be long and difficult, and he wasn't sure he was ready for it. But for the first time in years, Andrew felt the faint stirrings of something he thought he had lost forever: the will to live.

Part III: The Spiritual Awakening

Chapter 6: The Struggle to Let Go

Andrew B. sat in his car outside the small community center, his hands gripping the steering wheel so tightly his knuckles turned white. The parking lot was mostly empty, save for a few other cars scattered around, their drivers already inside the building. His heart raced as he stared at the unassuming front door. It looked so ordinary, but to him, it might as well have been a fortress, guarding everything he didn't want to face.

The past week had been a blur of hospital visits, doctor consultations, and uneasy sleep. His liver was still in critical condition, and his body was a wreck. But for once, his mind was sharp, free of the constant fog that alcohol had draped over his life. He hadn't had a drink in days—a victory that felt more like a curse as the cravings gnawed at him, reminding him how fragile his resolve truly was.

John's visit had shaken something loose inside him. The words from the *Big Book* had echoed in his mind since that night in the hospital. He had spent hours rereading the passages, trying to make sense of the stories of recovery, of surrender, of something greater than himself. And yet, even now, sitting here in the parking lot, he wasn't sure if he could go through with it.

He had built his life on control—on being the one in charge, the one others looked to for answers. Admitting that he was powerless felt like an admission of defeat, and that terrified him. The idea of surrendering to something beyond himself—whether it was a higher power or even just the recovery process—was foreign. But deep down, Andrew knew he couldn't keep going the way he had been. He had reached the end of himself.

With a deep breath, Andrew opened the car door and stepped out into the chilly evening air. He walked slowly toward the entrance, each step feeling heavier than the last. He had never been to a recovery meeting before, and the fear of the unknown clawed at his insides. What would these people think of him? Would they see through his carefully crafted facade, the one he had spent years building? Or worse, would they pity him?

Pushing the door open, Andrew stepped into the small room. It was modest, with a circle of folding chairs set up in the middle. A few people were already seated, chatting quietly among themselves. They looked ordinary—people from all walks of life, some dressed casually, others in work clothes. It was a far cry from the sterile hospital boardrooms or the polished galas he had once attended. Here, there were no pretenses. No masks.

Andrew hesitated at the entrance, unsure of where to sit or what to say. A man standing near the coffee table caught his eye and smiled. He was an older gentleman, his face weathered but kind. "First time?" he asked, his voice soft but reassuring.

Andrew nodded, unable to find the words.

"Welcome," the man said, motioning to an empty chair. "Grab a seat. We're glad you're here."

Andrew mumbled a thank you and sat down, his heart still racing. As more people filed in, the meeting began. A woman stood up, introducing herself as the chairperson for the evening. She welcomed everyone, especially the newcomers, and explained that they would start with readings from the *Big Book* and then move on to sharing.

As the words of the 12 Steps were read aloud, Andrew listened carefully, though his mind kept drifting. The concept of admitting powerlessness over alcohol—of turning his will and his life over to a higher power—felt like a foreign language. He was used to being the one who fixed things, who took control. How was he supposed to let go, especially when it felt like letting go would mean losing everything?

When the time for sharing came, Andrew's stomach knotted. He wasn't ready to speak, not yet. Instead, he listened as others began to tell their stories. Some spoke about years of sobriety, others about recent struggles with relapse. Each person was honest, raw, unguarded. There was no judgment in the room, just a sense of shared experience—people who understood the depths of addiction and the difficult path to recovery.

One man's story hit particularly close to home. He had been a successful lawyer before alcohol had destroyed his career and nearly cost him his family. As he talked about the denial, the pride, and the eventual crash that led him to seek help, Andrew saw himself in the man's words. The struggle for control, the refusal to admit defeat until everything had already been lost—it was all too familiar.

When the meeting ended, Andrew stayed in his chair, unsure of what to do next. He had expected to feel relief, but instead, he felt a rising frustration. The stories of recovery, of surrender, seemed impossible for him. How could he trust something greater than himself when he had never relied on anyone but himself? How could he let go when his entire life had been built on control?

As the others left the room, John, his old colleague, walked over and sat down beside him. "How are you feeling?" he asked.

Andrew shook his head, his voice barely above a whisper. "I don't know if I can do this."

John nodded, as if he had expected that response. "It's not easy," he said gently. "None of this is. Letting go of control feels impossible at first. But it's the only way."

"I don't even know where to start," Andrew admitted, the frustration bubbling to the surface. "I've spent my whole life fixing things—being in charge. And now, they're telling me I have to just... let go? How do you even do that?"

John smiled knowingly. "I thought the same thing when I first came here. I fought it every step of the way. But you don't have to understand it all right now. Just take it one day at a time. Start with Step One—admit that you're powerless. That's all. The rest will come in time."

Andrew sighed, feeling the weight of his resistance pressing down on him. The idea of surrender felt like failure, and his ego resisted every bit of it. But beneath that resistance, there was a glimmer of something else—something quieter, but no less powerful. Hope.

"I'll try," Andrew said, though the words felt uncertain. It wasn't much, but it was a start.

"Good," John replied. "That's all you need to do. Just try. And if you stumble, if you struggle, you come back. We're all in this together."

As Andrew left the meeting that night, he still felt the weight of his doubts and fears, but there was a small shift inside him. He had taken the first step, however reluctantly, and for the first time in years, he wasn't completely alone in his battle. The road to recovery stretched out before him, uncertain and filled with challenges, but for the first time, Andrew was willing to take that journey.

The struggle to let go would continue, and his ego would fight him every step of the way. But now, there was a chance—a small, flickering chance—that he could find his way back to himself. And maybe, just maybe, he could learn to trust in something greater than himself.

Chapter 7: A Glimmer of Hope

It had been a few months since Andrew B. first walked into that recovery meeting, his heart heavy with doubt and shame. The days that followed were some of the hardest he had ever faced. Each morning, he wrestled with the overwhelming urge to drink, the familiar craving that tugged at his mind and body like a relentless tide. There were moments when he nearly gave in, moments when the weight of sobriety felt too much to bear. But somehow, each time, he found himself back at the meetings, surrounded by people who understood his struggle.

The 12 Steps still felt like an impossible mountain to climb. Andrew had made it through the first few steps, admitting that he was powerless over alcohol and acknowledging that his life had become unmanageable. But surrendering to a higher power? That was still the step that stuck in his throat. He had always relied on logic, reason, and control. The idea of surrender—of trusting in something he couldn't see or touch—felt like a leap too far. Yet, despite his skepticism, he kept coming back. There was something about the stories he heard, the honesty of the people in those meetings, that gave him a glimmer of hope, even when he couldn't see the way forward.

One evening, after a particularly long day, Andrew found himself sitting alone in his apartment. The place was bare now, stripped of the warmth it had once held. Emily and the kids had left months ago, and the silence that filled the rooms was a constant reminder of everything he had lost. He had stayed sober, though—barely. The meetings were helping, but there were nights, like this one, when the urge to drink was almost unbearable.

As he sat on the couch, staring blankly at the TV, something inside him shifted. He had been fighting this battle for so long—fighting against alcohol, fighting against his own mind, fighting against the idea that he needed help. And for what? He had lost everything, and yet here he was, still trying to cling to control, still trying to fix things on his own.

Andrew stood up and walked to the window, looking out at the city below. The streets were quiet, the glow of streetlights casting long shadows on the pavement. For a long time, he just stood there, staring into the distance, his thoughts a swirling storm of regret and frustration. And then, in the quiet of that moment, something inside him broke.

It wasn't a sudden or dramatic realization, but rather a quiet surrender. He had been fighting for so long, resisting the very thing that could save him. And for the first time, Andrew understood—truly understood—that he couldn't do this alone. The fight had taken everything from him, and if he kept going this way, it would take his life as well.

He wasn't sure what he believed in. God, the universe, fate—it all felt abstract, distant. But as he stood there in the silence, Andrew felt something he hadn't felt in a long time: a presence, a sense of something greater than himself. It wasn't overwhelming or forceful, but rather a quiet, comforting feeling, like the gentle touch of a hand on his shoulder.

He didn't know what it was, but in that moment, Andrew realized he didn't have to. It didn't matter if he understood it fully. What mattered was that he couldn't beat this disease on his own—and maybe, just maybe, he didn't have to. For the first time, he allowed himself to consider the possibility that there was something out there—something bigger than his own ego and his own pain—that could help him heal.

Tears welled up in his eyes, and he let them fall. He had spent so many years trying to be strong, trying to hold it all together, but in this moment, he let go. He whispered a quiet prayer, though he wasn't even sure who or what he was praying to. "I can't do this alone," he said, his voice breaking. "Please help me."

It wasn't a grand epiphany or a bolt of lightning. There were no miracles, no immediate answers. But in the stillness of that moment, Andrew felt a sense of peace wash over him—a peace he hadn't known in years. It was as if the weight he had been carrying for so long had finally lifted, if only a little.

The next morning, Andrew returned to the meeting, feeling different. He still had doubts, still struggled with the idea of surrender. But something had changed inside him. For the first time, he was willing to let go—at least a little bit. He didn't have all the answers, and he didn't need them. All he knew was that he couldn't do this on his own, and for the first time, he was okay with that.

As the meeting began, Andrew listened more intently than ever before. When it came time for sharing, he spoke up, his voice steady but full of emotion. "I've been fighting this for so long," he said. "I've been trying to control everything—my drinking, my life, my family. And I've lost it all because of that. But last night, I realized something. I don't have to fight anymore. I don't know what I believe in, but I know I can't do this alone. So today, I'm letting go. I'm ready to trust the process, to trust something bigger than myself."

The room was silent for a moment, and then a wave of quiet understanding spread through the group. They had all been where Andrew was now—lost, afraid, uncertain. But they had found their way, one day at a time, by surrendering to the program, to the steps, and to something greater than themselves. And now, Andrew was ready to do the same.

In the weeks that followed, Andrew's commitment to the program deepened. He worked through the steps with a newfound sense of purpose, no longer resisting the idea of surrender but embracing it. He didn't have all the answers, and there were still days when the cravings hit hard, when the doubt crept back in. But now, he had something to hold onto—something bigger than his fears, his regrets, and his disease.

The spiritual awakening Andrew experienced that night wasn't the end of his journey—it was just the beginning. But it was the moment when he finally stopped fighting and started trusting. And with that trust came hope—a glimmer of hope that, no matter how broken his life had become, he could rebuild it. One step at a time. One day at a time.

Part IV: Building a New Life

Chapter 8: The Path to Recovery

The early days of Andrew B.'s recovery were some of the most difficult he had ever faced. Sobriety, though freeing, felt like walking on a tightrope. Each day was a balancing act between hope and fear, progress and temptation. The cravings for alcohol still came in waves—some days a faint whisper, others a roaring demand—but now, armed with the tools of the 12-Step Program, Andrew was learning how to navigate them.

He attended meetings regularly, often twice a day in the beginning. The rooms became his lifeline, a place where he could sit with others who understood the darkness he was fighting. His sponsor, a man named Greg, had been sober for nearly ten years and was patient, always reminding Andrew that recovery was a process—one that required persistence, humility, and an unshakable belief that he couldn't do it alone.

As he worked through the steps, Andrew found himself facing parts of his life he had long tried to avoid. Step Four—making a fearless moral inventory—forced him to confront the damage he had caused. He sat in his apartment one evening, a notebook in hand, listing every person he had hurt. Emily's name came first, followed by his children, then his colleagues, and eventually, his patients. The weight of his actions felt crushing. Years of lying, denial, and destruction stared back at him from the pages. It was overwhelming, but Andrew knew it was necessary. If he was ever going to rebuild his life, he had to start with the truth.

Step Five—admitting the exact nature of his wrongs—was equally humbling. He met with Greg in a quiet park, confessing the mistakes he had made. The lies he had told Emily, the times he had endangered patients, the friendships he had destroyed. As the words tumbled out, Andrew expected to feel shame, but instead, he felt a surprising sense of relief. The burden he had carried for so long was finally being shared, and in that sharing, he found release. Greg listened without judgment, nodding occasionally but mostly letting Andrew purge the guilt that had been festering inside him for years.

Step Nine—making amends—was the most daunting of all. It meant facing those he had hurt, owning up to his mistakes, and asking for forgiveness. Some conversations went better than others. His first attempt at making amends was with a former colleague, a nurse he had worked closely with during the height of his drinking. He remembered snapping at her one evening after she gently suggested that he was "off" during a surgery. Andrew had been defensive and rude, pushing her away when all she had tried to do was help. Now, standing outside the hospital where she still worked, Andrew felt a lump in his throat. But this was part of the process.

When she saw him, she was surprised but not unkind. Andrew explained why he was there, acknowledging the way he had treated her, admitting that his drinking had clouded his judgment and behavior. "I'm sorry," he said quietly. "I should have listened. You were only trying to help."

To his relief, she smiled softly and accepted his apology. "I knew something was wrong back then, but I didn't know how to help you," she said. "I'm glad you're getting better."

Some amends, however, were more painful. Facing Emily was the hardest of all. She had filed for divorce not long after she left, but Andrew had barely processed it. Now, sober for the first time in years, he saw the full extent of the damage he had caused. The broken promises, the nights she waited up for him, the moments he had missed with their children. It was all laid bare.

When they finally sat down together, Andrew struggled to find the words. "I'm sorry" felt so small compared to the hurt he had caused. But it was all he had.

"I've started making changes," he told her, his voice steady but full of emotion. "I'm working through the program, and I'm staying sober. But I know that doesn't erase everything I did."

Emily listened, her expression unreadable. When she finally spoke, her words were cautious but sincere. "I'm glad you're getting help, Andrew. But you have to understand... it's going to take time. A lot of time. You hurt us—me, the kids—and we can't just go back to the way things were."

Andrew nodded, knowing she was right. He wasn't asking for forgiveness overnight. He wasn't even sure if forgiveness would come at all. But he was willing to do the work, to show her that this time, he was serious.

Rebuilding his relationship with his children was another challenge. They had grown distant over the years, confused by his erratic behavior and hurt by his absence. Andrew began to reach out slowly, spending time with them when Emily allowed, showing up consistently to their events. He knew it would take time for them to trust him again, but each moment he spent with them—sober, present—felt like a step in the right direction.

Professionally, things were more complicated. The hospital had suspended him indefinitely after the incident in surgery, and while Andrew knew it would be a long road before he could practice medicine again, he was determined to make amends for the mistakes he had made. He wrote letters to the patients he had failed, expressing his remorse and commitment to recovery. Some responded with kindness, others with understandable anger, but Andrew knew that making amends wasn't about their reaction—it was about taking responsibility for his actions.

In the midst of all this, Andrew continued to battle the internal demons that had plagued him for so long. Triggers were everywhere—stressful moments that once would have sent him running for a drink now tested his resolve. Old habits lingered in the corners of his mind, waiting for a moment of weakness. But each time the cravings came, Andrew leaned on the tools he had learned in the program. He called his sponsor, went to a meeting, or sat quietly with his thoughts, acknowledging the urge without giving in to it.

There were days when the weight of sobriety felt too heavy to bear. Days when the enormity of the damage he had caused threatened to crush him. But in those moments, Andrew remembered what he had learned—one day at a time. He didn't have to solve everything at once. All he had to do was stay sober today.

As the weeks turned into months, Andrew began to see the slow, steady progress of his recovery. His relationship with Emily was still fragile, but they were talking more openly now. His children were warming up to him again, their laughter becoming more frequent during his visits. And while his professional life was still uncertain, he felt a renewed sense of purpose.

Recovery was not a straight path. It was full of ups and downs, moments of hope and moments of doubt. But Andrew had something now that he hadn't had before—a foundation. A belief that, with the help of the program, his higher power, and the people around him, he could rebuild his life, one step at a time.

And in that belief, there was a glimmer of something he hadn't felt in years: hope.

Chapter 9: Healing Others

Andrew B.'s life, once a whirlwind of chaos and destruction, had begun to settle into a quieter, more purposeful rhythm. After months of working through the 12 Steps, staying sober, and slowly rebuilding his relationships, he found himself in a place he had never imagined—contentment. It wasn't perfect, and there were still struggles, but the sense of despair that had haunted him for years had lifted. He had made it through the darkest part of his journey, and for the first time in a long time, Andrew felt hopeful not just for his future, but for the future of others like him.

One of the core principles of recovery was service to others, and now, with more than a year of sobriety behind him, Andrew was ready to take the next step. Greg, his sponsor, had been a guiding force throughout his recovery, always there to offer support and wisdom when Andrew needed it most. Now, Greg encouraged him to give back by sponsoring newcomers to the program.

At first, Andrew was hesitant. He still felt like a beginner in many ways, still wrestling with doubts and insecurities. How could he help others when he was still figuring things out himself? But Greg reminded him that sponsoring wasn't about having all the answers—it was about sharing the experience, strength, and hope he had gained along the way. It was about walking beside someone else in their journey, just as others had walked beside him.

With Greg's encouragement, Andrew agreed to sponsor his first newcomer—a man named Mark, who had recently joined the program. Mark was in the early stages of recovery, his life unraveling in ways that felt all too familiar to Andrew. He saw himself in Mark's weary eyes, the same fear and shame he had carried for so long. And though he wasn't sure how to start, Andrew knew that what Mark needed most was someone who had been there, someone who could listen without judgment and offer a path forward.

Their first meeting was at a coffee shop near the community center where the recovery meetings were held. Mark was nervous, fidgeting with his cup, unsure of what to say. Andrew understood that feeling well—the fear of opening up, of admitting how far you had fallen. He started by sharing his own story, not the polished version but the raw, painful truth of his descent into alcoholism and the long, hard road to sobriety.

As Andrew spoke, Mark began to relax. He asked questions, shared bits and pieces of his own story, and by the end of the meeting, the tension had eased. Mark wasn't alone anymore. He had someone who understood, someone who believed in him even when he didn't believe in himself.

Over the next few months, Andrew continued to sponsor Mark, guiding him through the early steps of the program, offering support during difficult moments, and celebrating the small victories. Each time they met, Andrew was reminded of his own journey—how far he had come and how much he had learned along the way. But more than that, he discovered a new sense of fulfillment in helping others. There was something deeply healing about being part of someone else's recovery, about witnessing the transformation that was possible when someone surrendered to the process.

As word spread within the recovery community, Andrew began to sponsor more people. He found himself becoming a mentor, not just to newcomers but to others who had been in the program for years but were still struggling. His background as a doctor gave him a unique perspective, allowing him to understand both the physical and emotional toll of addiction. But it was his personal experience—the years of pain, loss, and ultimately, redemption—that made his advice resonate.

In the process of helping others, Andrew felt himself healing in ways he hadn't expected. The service work wasn't just about keeping others sober—it was about keeping himself sober, too. Each time he sat down with a newcomer or attended a meeting, he was reminded of why he had chosen this path, of the life he had fought so hard to reclaim. And with each person he helped, the sense of purpose he had once found in medicine was reignited.

This newfound fulfillment began to shift Andrew's thinking about his professional life. The hospital had offered him the chance to return, but he wasn't sure if that was the path he wanted anymore. Surgery had once been his identity, but now, after everything he had been through, Andrew felt drawn to something different. Medicine was still a part of him, but so was his journey through addiction. He wanted to help people heal—not just physically, but emotionally and spiritually.

The idea of combining his medical background with addiction treatment began to take root. He started researching opportunities to work in recovery clinics, where he could use both his professional skills and his personal experience to help others. The more he explored, the more he realized how much his own story could serve others—not just as a doctor, but as someone who had walked the same path of darkness and found his way out.

Andrew reached out to a local addiction treatment center, inquiring about opportunities to work with recovering alcoholics and addicts. They welcomed him with open arms, recognizing the value of having a physician who not only understood the medical aspects of addiction but also the deeply personal struggle. He began volunteering there a few days a week, sitting in on group therapy sessions, offering medical advice, and sharing his story with patients who were at the beginning of their own recovery journeys.

The work was challenging, but it was also deeply rewarding. Andrew found himself connecting with patients in a way he never had as a surgeon. He wasn't just treating their symptoms—he was helping them rebuild their lives, piece by piece, just as he had done with his own.

As the months passed, Andrew's role at the treatment center grew. He became a full-time staff member, working closely with both the medical team and the recovery coaches to create holistic treatment plans for patients. He saw firsthand the impact of the 12 Steps, the power of community, and the importance of addressing both the physical and emotional aspects of addiction.

Andrew's life had taken a direction he never could have predicted. He had lost everything—his career, his family, his sense of self. But in the process of recovery, he had found something far more meaningful. He had found a new way to heal, not just himself, but others who were walking the same difficult path.

And in helping others heal, Andrew had finally found the one thing that had eluded him for so long: peace. Peace in knowing that his past didn't define him, and that even in the midst of his darkest moments, he had found a way to use his story to bring light to others.

His professional life might have changed, but his purpose had only deepened. He was still a healer, but now, it wasn't just his hands that did the work—it was his heart, his story, and his commitment to helping others find their way back to life.

Part V: Redemption and Service

Chapter 10: A Life Transformed

The early morning light filtered through the windows of the small recovery center as Andrew B. sat quietly in his office, reflecting on the long, winding road that had brought him here. The room was peaceful, a stark contrast to the chaos that had once dominated his life. Outside, patients gathered for their daily meeting, their laughter and conversation a reminder of the hope that permeated this place—a hope that Andrew himself had once struggled to find.

It had been years since he first walked into that recovery meeting, scared, ashamed, and uncertain if he could ever reclaim his life. Now, sitting here as a staff member at the very treatment center where he had once volunteered, Andrew saw the arc of his journey with a clarity that had eluded him for so long.

His life had changed in ways he never could have imagined. The man who had once been consumed by alcohol and driven by ego was now a humble servant in the recovery community. And while the pain of his past still lingered, it no longer defined him. Instead, it had become the foundation upon which his new life was built—a life of purpose, service, and peace.

As Andrew reflected on the darkest moments of his journey, he realized that those moments, painful as they were, had been necessary. They had stripped him of the illusions he had clung to for so long—the illusion of control, the illusion of perfection, and the illusion that he could face life's struggles alone. In losing everything, he had found something far more valuable: the truth that surrender, not control, was the path to freedom.

But even now, with years of sobriety behind him, Andrew knew the challenges of recovery were never truly over. Sobriety wasn't a destination; it was a daily commitment, a constant choice. There were still days when the old cravings resurfaced, triggered by stress or nostalgia. But unlike before, Andrew now had tools—real, tangible tools—that helped him navigate those moments without turning to alcohol.

He had learned to recognize the signs of relapse long before they took hold. When the pressure of life mounted, he reached for his phone to call his sponsor, attended a meeting, or spent time in quiet reflection. He no longer feared his own vulnerability; instead, he embraced it as part of the human experience. Where once he had seen his need for help as a weakness, he now understood it as a strength. Asking for help, relying on others, and leaning on his higher power were the things that kept him grounded, that kept him moving forward.

His spirituality had deepened over the years as well. Andrew's initial reluctance to embrace the idea of a higher power had given way to a quiet but profound sense of faith. He still wasn't sure what form that higher power took—whether it was God, the universe, or something else entirely—but that no longer mattered. What mattered was that he believed in something greater than himself, something that had carried him through the darkest days of his life and into the light of recovery.

He often reflected on the spiritual awakening he had experienced that night alone in his apartment, the moment when he had finally let go of control and allowed himself to surrender. That surrender had been the turning point, the beginning of his transformation. And now, as he sat here, years later, he could feel that same quiet presence guiding him—whispering to him in moments of doubt, offering peace in moments of chaos, and reminding him that he was never alone.

Helping others had become Andrew's lifeline, just as much as it had become theirs. Each day, he worked with men and women who were where he had once been—lost, broken, and desperate for a way out. He saw the pain in their eyes, the fear of confronting the truth, the shame of their past mistakes. But he also saw something else: the potential for healing, the flicker of hope that came from knowing they didn't have to face their struggles alone.

Andrew's work at the treatment center had grown over time. He now led group therapy sessions, facilitated workshops on addiction recovery, and mentored new staff members who shared his passion for helping others find sobriety. He was no longer just a doctor—he was a guide, a mentor, and a fellow traveler on the path of recovery. And in helping others heal, Andrew found a deeper sense of healing within himself.

There were moments, of course, when the weight of his past still pressed on him. He hadn't fully repaired his relationship with Emily, and the distance between them remained. But they were on better terms now, speaking more openly, co-parenting their children with respect and care. His children, who had once pulled away from him in fear and confusion, were slowly beginning to trust him again. He had learned that rebuilding trust was a process—one that took time, patience, and consistency. And he was willing to put in that time, no matter how long it took.

Professionally, Andrew's life had taken on new meaning. Medicine had always been his calling, but now, addiction treatment had become his passion. He was using both his medical knowledge and his personal experience to make a difference in the lives of others. He had found a balance between the two, integrating his past with his present in a way that felt authentic and fulfilling.

As Andrew looked out at the recovery center grounds, he felt a profound sense of gratitude wash over him. His life, once defined by chaos and pain, had transformed into something beautiful. He was no longer the man who had been swallowed by addiction. He was a man who had faced his demons, fought for his life, and emerged stronger on the other side.

There were still challenges, still days when the road felt long and difficult. But Andrew knew now that he didn't have to walk it alone. He had his higher power, his recovery community, and the tools he had gained through the 12 Steps. And with each passing day, he found a deeper sense of peace—a peace that came from knowing he had survived, that he had healed, and that he was helping others do the same.

As the morning light continued to fill the room, Andrew smiled to himself. His life wasn't perfect, but it was real. It was full of purpose and meaning in ways he had never imagined. And in that, he had found redemption—not just for himself, but for the lives he had touched along the way.

His journey was far from over, but for the first time in a long time, Andrew felt truly alive. And that, more than anything else, was the greatest gift of all.

Chapter 11: The Ripple Effect

Over the years, Andrew B.'s recovery had become more than just his personal journey—it had become a force of change that extended far beyond his own life. What had begun as a desperate struggle to reclaim himself had blossomed into something much larger, touching the lives of countless others in ways he could never have imagined.

One of the first people to feel the ripple effect of Andrew's transformation was Mark, the man Andrew had sponsored during the early days of his sobriety. Mark had come to the program with little hope, his life falling apart in much the same way Andrew's had years earlier. He had been drinking for decades, lost his family, and was on the verge of losing his job. Andrew saw the pain and fear in Mark's eyes and recognized it as his own. Over time, through their meetings and conversations, Mark began to change.

With Andrew's guidance, Mark worked through the steps, slowly rebuilding his life, one day at a time. He mended relationships with his children, who had written him off as a lost cause, and found the courage to pursue a job in social work, helping others who struggled with addiction. The transformation was profound, and Mark often credited Andrew's influence as the reason he hadn't given up when things seemed hopeless.

Years later, Mark stood in front of a room full of newcomers at a recovery meeting, sharing his story. "If it weren't for Andrew," he said, his voice steady, "I wouldn't be here today. He showed me that there was a way out, even when I didn't believe it. And now, I get to do the same for others."

Andrew had become a quiet, yet powerful, symbol of redemption in the recovery community. Word of his story spread beyond the walls of the treatment center and meetings. People came to him not just because he had been a doctor, but because he had been to the depths of despair and found a way out. He had once been the man who was broken, lost, and consumed by addiction, and now he was the man who offered hope to others.

One woman, Sara, had heard about Andrew from a mutual friend and sought him out during one of his workshops. She had been in and out of recovery programs for years, unable to maintain sobriety, feeling like she was doomed to fail. But something about Andrew's story resonated with her. When she finally spoke with him, she shared her fears—the fear that she would never be enough, that she would always fall back into her old habits.

Andrew listened, nodding with understanding. He knew those fears well. He told her that recovery wasn't about perfection or getting everything right. "It's about showing up, even when it feels impossible," he said. "One day at a time. You don't have to win the war today. Just focus on staying sober today."

Sara took his words to heart. She began attending meetings regularly, working through the 12 Steps with Andrew's encouragement. And when she stumbled—because everyone stumbles—Andrew was there, reminding her that recovery was about progress, not perfection. Over time, Sara found her footing. She celebrated her first year of sobriety surrounded by friends and family, a milestone she once thought she'd never reach. And like so many others, she pointed to Andrew as the person who had given her the strength to believe it was possible.

The stories kept coming. There was John, the young man who had lost his father to alcoholism and was on the verge of following the same path. After hearing Andrew speak at a local outreach event, John decided to check into a treatment program. Years later, John became a counselor himself, working with teenagers who struggled with addiction. "Andrew's story showed me that it didn't matter how far down you went," John often told his clients. "There's always a way back up."

Even Andrew's former colleagues, those who had once distanced themselves from him during his darkest days, began to see him in a new light. One of his old friends from the hospital, Dr. Rebecca Morgan, had watched Andrew's fall from grace with sadness but had never quite understood the depths of his struggle until she attended one of his talks on addiction recovery. Hearing him speak, Rebecca saw not just the broken man who had once lost everything, but the transformed individual who had rebuilt his life on honesty, humility, and service to others.

"I never thought I'd say this," Rebecca told him afterward, "but I'm proud of you, Andrew. You've done more good in the past few years than most people do in a lifetime."

Andrew's transformation had also rippled out into his family. Though his relationship with Emily remained complicated, there was healing. They had found a new way of relating to one another, co-parenting their children with mutual respect and, in time, friendship. His children, once distant, now sought out their father for advice and support. He had missed so much of their lives during his years of drinking, but now, sober, he was present for them in ways that mattered most. And while their trust hadn't been fully restored overnight, they were slowly beginning to see him as the father they had needed all along.

Through all of this, Andrew remained humble. He knew that his recovery, while hard-earned, was not a solitary victory. It was the result of community, of grace, and of surrender to something greater than himself. He had not arrived at some final destination of enlightenment. Recovery, he knew, was not a straight line; it was a winding, lifelong journey that required vigilance, commitment, and a willingness to show up every single day.

There were still challenges. There were still moments when the cravings surfaced or when life threw unexpected stress his way. But now, Andrew had the tools to navigate those moments. He had his recovery community, his higher power, and the knowledge that he didn't have to face life's struggles alone.

As he reflected on his journey, Andrew often thought about the ripple effect of recovery—the way one person's transformation could touch the lives of so many others. He had started his journey fighting for his own survival, but along the way, he had discovered that healing was not just about himself. It was about sharing that healing with others, offering hope where there had once been only despair.

Recovery had taught him that redemption wasn't something that came all at once—it came in small moments of grace, in the decision to stay sober one more day, and in the quiet acts of service that made a difference in the lives of others. It came in the recognition that life, with all its pain and joy, was worth living fully, sober, and present.

As Andrew watched the sun set over the recovery center one evening, he smiled to himself. His journey wasn't over, and it never would be. Recovery was not a destination to reach but a path to walk, one step at a time, for the rest of his life. And in walking that path, he had found peace—not just for himself, but for the countless others who had found hope in his story.

And that, Andrew knew, was what made the journey worthwhile.

Epilogue: A Doctor's Legacy

Andrew B. sat on the porch of his modest home, the late afternoon sun casting long shadows across the yard. The air was crisp, filled with the scents of autumn, and the quiet hum of the neighborhood around him felt peaceful. It was the kind of peace that had once eluded him for years—a peace he hadn't even known was possible when he was consumed by his addiction. Now, it was a part of him, woven into the fabric of his life, just as much as the struggles and triumphs that had brought him here.

As he sipped his coffee, Andrew thought about the road he had traveled. He had once been a man defined by his achievements—a brilliant surgeon, successful by all outward appearances, yet hollow inside. The ambition and drive that had fueled his medical career had also led him to the brink of destruction, and for a long time, he had believed that his legacy would be one of failure, defined by the dark spiral of alcoholism that had nearly claimed his life.

But now, years removed from that darkness, Andrew understood something he hadn't grasped before: his alcoholism, though destructive, had been part of a larger journey—a journey that had forced him to confront the parts of himself he had spent years running from. It had broken him down, but in the breaking, it had also offered him the opportunity to rebuild, not just as a doctor, but as a human being.

Looking back, Andrew realized that the addiction wasn't just something that had happened to him; it had shaped him in profound ways. It had pushed him to seek answers beyond the surface, to look inward and find a deeper connection with himself, his spirituality, and the people around him. Through the pain and suffering, he had found a sense of purpose that went far beyond the operating room.

His medical career had once been his defining achievement, the measure of his success. But now, Andrew knew that his true legacy lay in something much more meaningful. It wasn't in the surgeries he had performed or the accolades he had received, but in the lives he had touched through his recovery journey. The people he had sponsored, the patients he had helped in the treatment center, the individuals who had found hope because he had once found his way back from the edge—those were the legacies that truly mattered.

Andrew's story had become a source of inspiration for many. Not because he had been a great surgeon, but because he had been willing to face his own brokenness, to surrender to the process of recovery, and to extend his hand to others who were struggling. His life had become a testament to the power of transformation, to the idea that even in our darkest moments, we can find light if we are willing to reach for it.

The ripple effect of his recovery had extended far beyond what he had ever imagined. People in the community saw him as a beacon of hope, someone who had once been lost but had found his way back, someone who offered proof that redemption was possible, no matter how far one had fallen. And Andrew took that responsibility seriously. He continued to sponsor newcomers, to speak at meetings, and to mentor those who needed guidance on their own paths to recovery.

But more than that, Andrew had found a sense of peace within himself—a peace that came from understanding that life was not about perfection, but about progress. He had learned to forgive himself for the mistakes of the past, to let go of the need for control, and to embrace the uncertainty of life with a sense of grace and humility.

His relationship with his family had healed over time. Emily had moved on with her own life, but they had found a way to co-exist peacefully, co-parenting their children with mutual respect and kindness. His children, now older, had begun to see him not as the man who had once let them down, but as the father who had worked hard to earn back their trust. Their love and forgiveness had been one of the greatest gifts of his recovery, a reminder that healing was possible, even in the most fractured relationships.

As the sun dipped lower on the horizon, Andrew thought about the future. He knew that his journey wasn't over. Recovery was a lifelong process, one that required constant attention and care. But now, instead of fearing that journey, he welcomed it. He had learned that life was not about reaching a destination, but about walking the path with an open heart, a clear mind, and a willingness to grow.

Andrew's legacy, he realized, was not the sum of his achievements or the title of "doctor" he had once held so tightly. His legacy was in the hope he had spread, the lives he had touched, and the peace he had found within himself. It was in the quiet moments of service, in the conversations he had with those who were still struggling, and in the knowledge that his story had the power to make a difference.

As he stood up from the porch and took one last look at the setting sun, Andrew smiled. His life had taken turns he never could have predicted, but in the end, it had brought him to a place of deep understanding. He was at peace with his past, grateful for the present, and open to whatever the future might hold.

In his heart, he knew that the work of recovery, both for himself and for others, was never truly finished. It was a journey that would continue, one day at a time, for the rest of his life. And that, he thought, was the greatest legacy he could leave behind.

A life transformed, a story shared, and hope spread to those who needed it most. That was his true legacy—a doctor's legacy of healing, not just through medicine, but through love, service, and recovery.

The Third Step: Finding Light in the Darkness

Prologue: The Hospital Bed

The sterile smell of antiseptic filled the air, a faint buzz from the fluorescent lights overhead adding to the quiet hum of the hospital room. Ethan C. lay motionless in the bed, his body weak, his spirit broken. His once strong, confident frame now seemed frail, barely recognizable compared to the man he used to be. The IV line dripped slowly into his veins, a stark reminder of how far he had fallen. The doctors had said it before, and now, once again, the verdict was the same: there was no hope left for him.

He stared at the ceiling, his eyes bloodshot and sunken, every breath a painful reminder of the damage he had done. His liver was failing, his organs on the brink of collapse. And yet, the greatest pain wasn't physical. It was the hollow ache deep inside, the knowledge that he had lost everything to a bottle—his family, his career, his dignity. His wife had left him months ago, taking their children with her. Friends had drifted away, and the colleagues who had once admired him no longer returned his calls.

Ethan had tried to quit drinking before—so many times, in fact, that he had lost count. He had promised himself, promised his wife, promised his children that each time would be the last. But the promises always broke, just like his resolve. Each failed attempt only plunged him deeper into the abyss. He was no longer in control, if he had ever been. The drink controlled him, and he had resigned himself to the inevitable: alcohol would be his undoing.

He shifted slightly in the bed, his body too weak to do much more. He could hear the faint murmur of the nurses outside the room, talking about him, no doubt. He was the hopeless case. The man who couldn't be saved. The doctors had told him, just like all the others before: *Your body can't take this much longer. You're at the end of the line.*

But the truth was, Ethan had felt at the end of the line long before this hospital stay. It had been a slow, painful descent into darkness, and now, lying here, he wondered how much further there was to go. His thoughts wandered back to a time when his life had looked different. He had once been a successful businessman, respected in his field, with a wife and two children who adored him. The world had been his oyster, full of possibilities.

He had it all—or so he thought.

He had never imagined that something as simple as a drink could tear it all apart. It had started innocently enough—drinks at work functions, a few to unwind after a long day. But slowly, the line between social drinking and dependence blurred. What had once been an occasional escape from stress became a daily ritual, and before long, alcohol was the only thing that made the days bearable. It numbed him, took away the pain, the anxiety, the fear of failure.

But it had also taken away everything else.

As the drinking worsened, so did his life. He stopped showing up for work, let his business fall apart. His marriage crumbled under the weight of his lies and broken promises. His children, once his pride and joy, grew distant, afraid of the man their father had become. He had tried to hold it together, but the more he tried to fight, the tighter alcohol's grip became.

Now, there was nothing left to fight for. His body was giving up, and he had resigned himself to the fact that this was how his story would end. There were no more promises to make, no more lies to tell. There was just him, alone in this hospital bed, waiting for the inevitable.

The sound of footsteps approaching broke the silence. Ethan didn't bother to look up. It was probably another nurse, coming to check his vitals, maybe even a doctor ready to deliver the same grim prognosis he'd heard a dozen times before. But when the door opened, the voices he heard weren't those of medical staff.

"Is this Ethan C.?" a calm voice asked.

Ethan turned his head slowly, his curiosity piqued. Two men stood at the foot of his bed. They didn't wear white coats or scrubs, and they didn't look like doctors or nurses. There was something different about them—something quiet, yet steady.

"Yes, that's him," one of the nurses replied, giving them a brief nod before slipping out of the room.

The men stepped closer, their eyes meeting Andrew's. For a moment, no one spoke. Then, the man who had spoken first, a tall, slightly graying figure, smiled warmly. "Hi, Andrew. My name's John, and this is Bill. We're here to talk to you about something that might help."

Andrew's eyes narrowed. *Help?* He had been offered help before—countless rehab centers, doctors, therapists—all telling him the same thing, and none of it had worked. What made these men any different?

But there was something in the way they looked at him. Something that felt familiar. They didn't look at him with pity or judgment, but with understanding. As if they had been exactly where he was now.

"We know what you're going through," Bill said quietly. "We've been where you are. We're both alcoholics too."

Andrew's heart skipped a beat. *Alcoholics?* He had heard that word thrown around so many times by doctors and family, but never by someone who was admitting it themselves. These men were here to help *him*, but they were also like him?

John spoke again, his voice steady but kind. "We know how hard this is. We know it feels hopeless. But we're living proof that there's a way out."

Ethan wanted to scoff, to roll his eyes at the idea that these strangers could possibly understand the depths of his despair. But as he looked at them, he saw something in their faces—something he hadn't seen in a long time: hope.

For the first time in years, a small flicker of curiosity sparked inside him. He didn't believe in miracles. He didn't believe in redemption. But these men, standing here in front of him, were offering something he hadn't expected.

A way out.

Ethan shifted in the bed, his voice barely more than a whisper. "Tell me more."

And so, as John and Bill sat beside him, sharing their stories of recovery, Ethan listened. For the first time in what felt like forever, he listened—not with skepticism, but with something else, something he hadn't felt in years.

A glimmer of hope.

And maybe, just maybe, that glimmer would be enough to start him on the path to a new life.

Part I: The Descent into Darkness

Chapter 1: A Promising Beginning

Ethan C.'s life began in a small Midwestern town, the kind of place where everyone knew each other, and hard work was the most valued currency. His father had been a factory worker, his mother a schoolteacher. From a young age, Ethan had been taught the importance of perseverance, responsibility, and ambition. His parents didn't have much, but they instilled in him the belief that with dedication and effort, he could achieve anything.

Ethan was bright and determined, excelling in school and sports, always pushing himself to be the best at whatever he did. His teachers spoke of his potential, calling him a natural leader. In high school, he was voted class president, and his academic achievements earned him a scholarship to a prestigious university. He studied business, knowing it would provide him with opportunities to make a name for himself.

At university, Andrew's drive only intensified. He threw himself into his studies, impressing professors with his sharp intellect and clear ambition. But it wasn't all work—he made friends easily and enjoyed the camaraderie that came with college life. Social events, parties, and networking functions were a regular part of the experience, and alcohol was always present.

Andrew's first encounters with alcohol were casual, a few beers at a football game or a couple of cocktails at networking events. Drinking was just something everyone did—an easy way to unwind after long study sessions or break the ice at social gatherings. He wasn't particularly drawn to alcohol at first, but he liked the way it loosened him up, made him more outgoing, more confident. Besides, it seemed harmless. He was always in control—smart enough not to let anything get in the way of his goals.

After graduating at the top of his class, Ethan was recruited by a large investment firm in the city. The job was everything he had worked for—high stakes, high rewards. The long hours were grueling, but Ethan thrived in the competitive atmosphere. He quickly gained a reputation as a rising star, someone who could handle pressure and deliver results.

As he climbed the corporate ladder, the social aspect of his career became even more important. Clients expected lavish dinners, drinks after meetings, and networking events that stretched late into the night. Ethan handled it all with ease—balancing work, networking, and the occasional drink with friends. Alcohol was a part of the lifestyle, but it was never a problem. He would have a few drinks, laugh with colleagues, and wake up the next morning ready to tackle another day.

As the years went by, though, the demands of his job began to take their toll. The pressure to succeed mounted with each promotion, and the weight of responsibility grew heavier. The stress was constant, and although Ethan was outwardly calm and collected, inside, the anxiety began to creep in. He found that a drink or two after work helped him relax. It took the edge off, dulled the worry that sometimes kept him awake at night. At first, it was just an occasional indulgence—a way to unwind after a particularly stressful day. But slowly, almost imperceptibly, it became a regular part of his routine.

Ethan didn't notice it at first, but his drinking began to shift. What had once been a casual way to relax became more of a necessity. He started having a drink when he got home, then another before bed to help him sleep. The next day, he'd shake it off, get through work, and do it all over again. He wasn't worried—he was still excelling at his job, still respected by his peers, still in control. But as the months passed, those two drinks after work turned into three, sometimes four.

The drinking was still manageable, at least in Andrew's mind. He wasn't getting drunk every night, just taking the edge off. Everyone drank—it was part of the culture, part of his life. And besides, he could quit whenever he wanted. He just didn't need to yet.

But the pressure at work continued to build, and Ethan began to rely on alcohol more and more. The social drinking that had once been confined to weekends and networking events became a nightly routine. He told himself it was normal—he was just blowing off steam after long hours at the office. But deep down, something had shifted. Alcohol wasn't just a way to relax anymore—it was becoming a crutch.

His personal life began to reflect the subtle changes. His wife, Emma, whom he had married a few years after his career took off, noticed that Ethan seemed distant, more irritable than he used to be. They had once shared dinners together, talking about their days and planning their future, but now Ethan spent more time at work or in his study, a glass of whiskey in hand. Emma expressed her concern, gently at first, but Ethan brushed it off. He was just stressed, he told her. The firm was demanding more of him, and he needed to keep up. The drinking wasn't a problem. He had it under control.

But over the years, the slide continued. His work performance began to suffer—missed deadlines, forgotten meetings, careless mistakes. His colleagues noticed that he wasn't as sharp as he used to be, though they never said it outright. Emma grew more worried, and their relationship began to strain under the weight of his increasing absence, both physically and emotionally. The drinking became more frequent, more necessary, though Ethan refused to acknowledge it.

He was still functioning—at least on the surface. He still went to work, still maintained a social life, still convinced himself that everything was fine. But inside, he knew something was wrong. The nights of drinking blurred together, and the days became harder to get through without it. What had once been a promising beginning was slowly unraveling, and Andrew, despite his best efforts to deny it, was slipping deeper into a world where alcohol was no longer a choice—it was a need.

And though he couldn't see it yet, this slow slide was taking him toward a darkness from which it would take everything to escape.

Chapter 2: The Turning Point

It wasn't any single event that marked Ethan C.'s descent into full-blown addiction. Instead, it was a series of small, gradual shifts that, over time, began to spiral out of control. What had once been an occasional drink to take the edge off became a regular fixture in his life. And then, before he realized it, alcohol had wrapped its grip around him, suffocating everything else.

Andrew's mornings now began with the lingering fog of a hangover. The first few hours of the workday were spent nursing coffee, trying to shake off the dull ache in his head, while hiding his exhaustion behind a façade of professionalism. But as the demands of his job mounted, so too did his reliance on alcohol. What had once been a way to unwind after work soon bled into lunchtime drinks, then afternoon meetings, where he subtly nursed cocktails or glasses of wine.

His colleagues noticed the changes, though they said nothing at first. Andrew's sharpness had dulled, and his once quick-witted responses in meetings were replaced by hesitations and absentmindedness. Small mistakes began to pile up—forgotten appointments, missed deadlines, financial projections that didn't add up. His boss, who had once praised Ethan for his tenacity, started asking questions. Subtly at first: *Are you feeling alright? Need some time off?*

But Ethan brushed it off. He could handle it. He was just going through a rough patch, that's all. Everyone goes through slumps, right? He told himself that his drinking was still under control, that it wasn't the problem. It was just stress from work, stress from his marriage, stress from life. *The drinking helps me manage it all,* he thought. *I can stop anytime I want.*

But that lie was unraveling faster than he could keep up with.

One evening, after an especially grueling day at the office, Ethan found himself at a bar downtown, a familiar escape from the pressures of home and work. He told himself he'd only have one drink, just to relax before heading home. But one drink turned into two, then three, then more. By the time he finally stumbled out of the bar, hours had passed, and the world around him was a blur of streetlights and car horns.

He had driven home drunk before, though he never admitted it to himself. Tonight was no different. Slipping into the driver's seat of his car, he fumbled with the keys, his hands trembling from the alcohol coursing through his veins. The drive was short, but in his intoxicated state, it felt like an eternity. He weaved in and out of traffic, narrowly avoiding collisions, his mind too clouded to recognize the danger he was in.

And then it happened.

A flash of red and blue lights in the rearview mirror. The siren blared, cutting through the haze of his drunken mind. Andrew's stomach dropped as the realization hit him—he was being pulled over.

The officer's face was grim as he approached the car. Ethan fumbled through excuses, slurring his words, trying to act as if everything was fine. But it was no use. The smell of alcohol was thick on his breath, and after a failed sobriety test, the cuffs were on his wrists, cold and heavy, as he was escorted to the back of the police car. For the first time, the consequences of his drinking became real.

Emma came to bail him out of jail the next morning. Her face was pale, a mixture of disappointment and exhaustion etched in her features. She had always suspected that Andrew's drinking was a problem, but now there was no denying it. As they drove home in silence, the tension between them felt unbearable.

When they finally reached the house, Emma confronted him. "You need help, Andrew," she said, her voice shaking. "This has gone too far. You could have killed someone. You could have ruined everything."

Ethan sat there, rubbing his temples, trying to block out the guilt and the shame that surged through him. "I know," he mumbled. "I'll stop. I promise."

But promises were something Ethan had become too good at breaking.

He tried. For the next few weeks, he cut back on drinking, throwing himself into work in an attempt to make up for lost time. But the damage had already been done. His boss had heard about the DUI, and the rumors about his declining performance were spreading through the office. His colleagues, once friendly and supportive, now kept their distance, whispering behind closed doors about his erratic behavior.

At home, things were worse. Emma had lost faith in his promises, and their arguments grew more frequent, more bitter. Ethan tried to show her that he was making an effort—drinking less, being more present—but the tension lingered. The drinking, though less frequent, never truly stopped. He would go days without touching a drop, convincing himself that he was regaining control, only to fall back into old habits after a particularly stressful day.

The breaking point came one night when Emma found him passed out on the living room couch, an empty bottle of whiskey on the floor beside him. It wasn't the first time she had seen him like this, but something had changed. She had reached her limit.

"I can't do this anymore, Andrew," she said, her voice thick with tears. "I can't keep pretending that everything is fine. You're destroying yourself, and I'm watching it happen."

Ethan barely registered her words, the alcohol dulling his senses. But when she packed a suitcase and left with their two children that night, the reality of his situation finally began to sink in. He had lost them. The people who mattered most in his life were gone, and it was because of him—because of the alcohol.

He made a half-hearted attempt to quit drinking after that. He swore to himself that he would stop, that this time it would be different. He tried willpower, avoiding bars, dumping bottles down the sink. But each time, the cravings crept back in, stronger than before. After a few days, the anxiety would build, the pressure would mount, and the cycle would start all over again.

Each relapse filled him with more shame, more self-loathing. He had tried everything he knew—cutting back, quitting cold turkey, switching from whiskey to beer, all the tricks he could think of. But nothing worked. The addiction had its claws in him, and no matter how hard he tried to claw his way out, it pulled him deeper.

The drinking intensified, and the consequences followed. He lost his job at the firm, his boss reluctantly letting him go after months of declining performance and missed deadlines. His legal issues mounted as the DUI charges lingered over him, a constant reminder of how far he had fallen. His friends stopped calling, stopped checking in. His family, distant and heartbroken, barely spoke to him anymore.

Ethan was spiraling, and though he knew it, he couldn't stop. Each attempt to quit was met with failure, and each failure drove him further into the bottle. The once-promising life he had built was crumbling before his eyes, and all he could do was watch as it fell apart.

It was in the middle of one of those dark nights, alone in his empty house, that Ethan finally admitted the truth to himself.

He couldn't do this on his own.

The alcohol had won.

And in that moment, as the weight of his failure crashed down on him, Ethan realized he was out of options. He had tried everything, but none of it had worked. He was lost, and the only thing he knew for certain was that if something didn't change soon, he would lose far more than just his job and his family.

He would lose himself.

Chapter 3: Hitting Rock Bottom

Ethan C. had never imagined his life would end up like this. He had once been the golden boy—a man with ambition, talent, and the world at his feet. Now, he was nothing more than a shadow of that person, lying in a hospital bed, waiting for the next bit of bad news from the doctors. His body, once strong and full of vitality, was failing. His liver was in ruins, his heart was weak, and his mind—dulled by years of alcohol abuse—was barely able to hold on to any hope.

This wasn't his first time in the hospital. It had become a cycle over the past few years: drinking until his body gave out, being rushed to the emergency room, going through detox, swearing to the doctors that he'd never drink again, and then finding himself back at the bar within days. Each time, the consequences grew worse. Each time, the recovery was slower. Each time, the promises meant less.

Now, lying in that hospital bed, Ethan felt the crushing weight of finality. The doctors weren't optimistic. They had done what they could, but the years of abuse had taken their toll. His liver was on the verge of failure, his body no longer able to process the constant stream of poison he had poured into it. The damage was irreversible. One of the doctors, a man with a somber face and a heavy heart, had told him bluntly, "If you keep drinking, Andrew, you won't survive the next time."

Those words echoed in his head, but even they felt distant now. He had heard similar warnings before, but somehow this time felt different. There was a grim finality in the doctor's tone, and deep down, Ethan knew he was right. He was running out of time.

He stared at the ceiling, the antiseptic smell of the hospital clinging to his senses. Machines beeped quietly around him, reminding him that his life was now sustained by technology, not by his own strength. He was weak, barely able to sit up on his own. His skin had a jaundiced tint, his eyes dull and bloodshot, his once-athletic frame reduced to a gaunt figure that seemed to fade more with each passing day.

There was no one left to visit him. His wife, Emma, had given up long ago. She had tried—oh, how she had tried—to help him, to save him from himself. But after years of broken promises, nights spent waiting for him to come home, and tearful arguments that always ended in disappointment, she had taken their children and left. It had been months since Ethan had last seen them, and even longer since he had spoken to them.

His friends, too, had drifted away. At first, they had tried to pull him back, encouraging him to quit drinking, offering support when he needed it most. But Ethan had pushed them all away, consumed by his addiction, unwilling to admit that he needed help. Now, there was no one left. His phone hadn't rung in weeks, and the only people who knew he was in the hospital were the doctors and nurses who checked in on him during their rounds.

Ethan was alone.

He had lost his job a long time ago, after one too many missed meetings and an embarrassing incident at a client dinner where he had shown up visibly drunk. The firm had given him chance after chance, but eventually, even they couldn't ignore the obvious. He was unreliable, a liability, and they let him go with a severance package that barely covered his growing debts. His savings had long since dried up, and his once-comfortable lifestyle had been reduced to a meager existence in a rundown apartment he could barely afford.

But it wasn't the loss of his job, his wife, or even his health that weighed on him most heavily. It was the loss of his self-respect. Ethan had always prided himself on being in control, on being the kind of man who could handle whatever life threw at him. But now, that control was gone. Alcohol had stripped him of his dignity, leaving him broken and powerless.

As he lay in the hospital bed, staring blankly at the ceiling, Ethan felt the crushing weight of his isolation. He had no one left to turn to, no one who could pull him out of the darkness he had fallen into. The doctors had made it clear: if he didn't stop drinking, he would die. But even now, with death looming over him, Ethan wasn't sure if he could stop. He had tried—countless times—and each attempt had ended in failure. Willpower wasn't enough. Nothing was enough.

The realization hit him like a wave. He couldn't do it. He had lost the battle. The addiction was stronger than he was, and it had won. For the first time, Ethan faced the truth that had been staring him in the face for years: he was powerless over alcohol. He had no control, no ability to stop on his own. He had tried everything—rehab, counseling, self-help books—but nothing had worked.

He was trapped in a cycle he couldn't break.

Tears welled up in his eyes, but he was too exhausted to cry. He felt empty, as if the alcohol had drained not only his body but his soul. There was no more fight left in him. He had hit rock bottom, and the thought of trying to climb out felt impossible.

Ethan closed his eyes, his mind drifting through the memories of his life—the promise of his youth, the success of his early career, the love he had once shared with Emma, the laughter of his children. All of it was gone, replaced by the hollow void of addiction. He had nothing left. No future, no hope, no escape.

The doctor's words echoed in his mind once more: *If you keep drinking, Andrew, you won't survive the next time.*

And yet, as he lay there, broken and defeated, he wasn't sure if he wanted to survive. What was left for him in this world? The thought of trying to rebuild his life felt overwhelming, the idea of facing the people he had hurt unbearable. It would be easier to let go, to surrender to the disease that had taken everything from him.

But somewhere, deep within that darkness, a small flicker of something stirred. It wasn't hope, not yet, but it was something close.

A whisper, barely audible, reminding him that maybe—just maybe—there was another way. Maybe this didn't have to be the end.

Ethan didn't know what that other way looked like, or if he even had the strength to find it. But as the hospital room fell silent around him, he realized that he wasn't ready to give up just yet.

Not completely.

There was still something inside him that wanted to fight, that wanted to believe there was a way out. And maybe, if he could find it, there was still a chance—however small—that he could reclaim the life he had lost.

For the first time in a long time, Ethan allowed himself to wonder: *What if this wasn't the end? What if, somehow, there was a way to begin again?*

But as the darkness closed in around him, he knew one thing for sure: he couldn't do it alone. Not anymore. If he was going to find his way back, he would need help.

Real help.

And for the first time in years, Ethan allowed himself to consider that maybe—just maybe—help was possible.

If only he could find the courage to ask for it.

Part II: The First Spark of Hope

Chapter 4: Meeting Alcoholics Anonymous

Ethan lay in his hospital bed, staring blankly at the wall as the dull hum of machines buzzed around him. He had heard the doctor's words clearly: his body was barely holding on. If he didn't stop drinking, he wouldn't live to see another year, maybe even another month. But it wasn't the first time Ethan had heard a dire prognosis. He had been told before that he needed to quit drinking—by doctors, therapists, and even Emma, before she left. But none of it had made a difference. He had tried to stop, really tried, but no matter what he did, he always ended up back where he started—drunk, broken, and alone.

So when two men walked into his hospital room that afternoon, Ethan didn't bother to lift his head. He assumed they were more doctors or nurses, coming to deliver the same tired speech about detox programs or medications that might help.

But these men weren't doctors. They weren't wearing white coats or carrying clipboards. They were dressed casually, and their faces were kind but serious. The first man, slightly older with graying hair, stepped forward, his hand extended.

"Hi, Andrew. My name's Bill, and this is John. We're here to talk to you about something that helped us. Something we think might help you too."

Ethan turned his head slightly, his eyes narrowing. *Help me?* He had heard that before. He had been in and out of rehab facilities, gone through countless treatments. Nothing had worked. These men, whoever they were, couldn't possibly understand the depths of what he was going through. How could they?

Bill and John pulled up chairs and sat down next to the bed, their movements calm and deliberate. They weren't in a rush, and they didn't seem like they were here to lecture him. They just sat, quietly, waiting for him to say something.

"What do you want?" Ethan finally asked, his voice hoarse and dry. He felt weak, physically and mentally. The alcohol had drained everything from him, leaving him a hollow shell.

"We're from Alcoholics Anonymous," Bill said simply. "We've been where you are. We've hit bottom, just like you. And we wanted to share our stories with you. Maybe something will resonate. Maybe not. But we thought it was worth a try."

Andrew's eyes narrowed further. Alcoholics Anonymous. He had heard about it before, of course. He had seen the name mentioned in brochures and on the lips of therapists, but he had never taken it seriously. It sounded like another self-help group, another set of promises that wouldn't work for someone like him. Still, there was something about the way Bill spoke—calm, assured—that made him pause. These men weren't here to sell him something, and they weren't judging him.

"Yeah, well, I've heard it all before," Ethan muttered, turning his face away. "Nothing works for me."

John leaned forward slightly, his voice soft but firm. "I used to think that too," he said. "I spent years trying to quit drinking on my own. I went through hospitals, detox centers, the works. I kept telling myself I could fix it, that I didn't need help. But the truth is, I was powerless. The alcohol had me, just like it has you. And until I admitted that, until I stopped trying to fight it on my own, nothing changed."

Ethan blinked, still staring at the wall. He didn't respond, but he was listening. Something in John's words felt familiar. The idea of being powerless wasn't new, but hearing someone else say it, someone who claimed to have been where he was, made it feel more real. Still, he couldn't bring himself to believe that there was a way out for him. He had tried so many times, and each failure had only driven him deeper into despair.

"I've tried," Ethan whispered. "I've tried everything. Nothing works."

Bill leaned back in his chair, his expression thoughtful. "I get it," he said. "I tried everything too. But Alcoholics Anonymous isn't about willpower or trying harder. It's about surrender. It's about admitting that we can't do this alone, that we need help from something greater than ourselves. And that's when things started to change for me."

"Surrender?" Ethan repeated, a bitter laugh escaping his lips. "What's that supposed to mean? I've already lost everything. I've got nothing left."

John smiled gently. "That's the thing, Andrew. You don't have to lose everything to surrender. You just have to let go of the idea that you can fix this by yourself. You're not alone in this. There's a whole fellowship of people who have been through what you're going through. And they've found a way out, together."

Andrew's mind raced, though his body remained still. Could it really be that simple? Just surrender? Let go of the fight? He had always believed that he had to fix himself, that if he just tried hard enough, if he was strong enough, he could beat this. But maybe that was the problem. Maybe he had been fighting the wrong battle all along.

Still, doubt clouded his thoughts. He had heard promises before, and each time they had led to more disappointment. What made Alcoholics Anonymous any different? How could he trust these men who claimed to understand him, to have found a solution?

"I don't know," Ethan finally said, his voice quiet. "I don't know if I can believe any of this. I've been down this road too many times."

Bill nodded, not pushing. "We're not asking you to believe everything right away," he said. "Just think about it. Come to a meeting. Listen to the stories. See if anything resonates with you. That's all we're asking. Just one small step."

Ethan stayed silent, his mind spinning. He wasn't sure he could trust himself to take even that small step. But as he glanced at the two men sitting calmly beside him, sharing their stories with no judgment or expectation, he felt something stir inside him. It wasn't hope, not yet. But it was something. A tiny flicker of curiosity, a question he hadn't dared to ask in a long time: *What if?*

What if these men were right? What if there was a way out? What if he didn't have to do this alone?

Ethan didn't have the answers. He didn't know if he could find the strength to show up at one of those meetings, or if he could ever trust himself to recover. But for the first time in a long time, he considered the possibility that maybe, just maybe, there was something more for him.

As Bill and John stood to leave, Bill offered one final thought. "Just remember, Andrew—this isn't about fixing everything overnight. It's about taking it one day at a time. That's how we did it. And if you're willing, that's how you can do it too."

They left a pamphlet on the table next to his bed, a simple brochure with the words "Alcoholics Anonymous" printed across the top. Ethan glanced at it briefly before turning his gaze back to the ceiling. He wasn't sure what his next step would be, but for the first time in a long time, he felt the tiniest seed of change take root inside him.

Maybe there was a way out.

Maybe he wasn't beyond help after all.

Chapter 5: Surrender

The pamphlet sat on the bedside table, untouched for days after Bill and John's visit. Ethan didn't want to look at it. He didn't want to face the possibility that maybe, just maybe, those two men had been right. Alcoholics Anonymous sounded like another empty promise, another fleeting solution in a long list of failed attempts. But the words they had spoken continued to echo in his mind: *You can't do this alone. Surrender.*

The word *surrender* made Ethan uncomfortable. He had spent his entire life trying to be strong, trying to control every aspect of his world. He had built his career, his family, his life on the idea that if he worked hard enough, pushed himself far enough, he could overcome anything. But now, lying in the hospital bed, his body wrecked by alcohol, Ethan began to see that his battle with drinking was different. No amount of strength or willpower had ever been enough to stop the downward spiral.

One afternoon, as he stared out the window, Ethan felt something shift inside him. It wasn't a grand revelation or a moment of dramatic clarity. It was more like a quiet acceptance—a realization that he had been fighting a losing battle. He couldn't control this. He had tried, and he had failed. Over and over again. For the first time, Ethan allowed himself to admit the one thing he had never wanted to face: *I can't do this alone.*

That night, after the nurses left him to rest, Ethan picked up the pamphlet from the table. He turned it over in his hands, running his fingers along the smooth paper. The words "Alcoholics Anonymous" stood out in bold print, but it wasn't the title that caught his attention. It was the simple message written underneath: *One day at a time.*

Ethan didn't know much about Alcoholics Anonymous, but something about that phrase resonated with him. It wasn't asking him to fix everything overnight. It wasn't demanding that he change his entire life in an instant. It was asking him to take it *one day at a time*. That, he thought, maybe he could do.

The next morning, Ethan called the number Bill had left him.

When Bill answered, Andrew's voice was hesitant, almost shaky. "I've been thinking," he said slowly, "about what you and John told me. I... I don't know if I believe it will work, but I'm willing to try. I don't have anything else left."

There was a pause on the other end of the line before Bill spoke, his voice calm and reassuring. "That's all you need right now, Andrew. Just the willingness to try. We'll take it from there."

Bill arranged to meet Ethan the next day, offering to take him to his first A.A. meeting. As the time drew closer, Andrew's nerves kicked in. He wasn't sure what to expect. Would it be like all the other programs he had tried? Was it just another false hope? Doubts gnawed at him, but something deeper, something quieter, pushed him to follow through. He couldn't explain it, but there was a sense of calm under the surface, a sense that maybe this was the first step he needed to take.

The meeting was held in the basement of a small church on the edge of town. When Bill pulled up in his car to take him, Ethan felt the familiar pang of anxiety in his chest. He had never been the type to ask for help, let alone walk into a room full of strangers to admit that he had a problem he couldn't solve. But Bill's presence was steady, and as they walked into the meeting together, Ethan felt his nerves begin to settle.

The room was simple, with folding chairs arranged in a circle. About a dozen people were already seated, chatting quietly before the meeting began. Ethan noticed that they looked like ordinary people—men and women of all ages, from all walks of life. There was no judgment in their eyes, no pity. Instead, they greeted him warmly, introducing themselves with smiles and nods.

Bill sat beside him and leaned in. "Just listen," he said quietly. "You don't have to say anything. Just listen to their stories."

The meeting began with a few readings from the *Big Book*, and Ethan felt a sense of unease creeping in. He wasn't sure about the spiritual aspect of A.A., and the idea of turning his will over to a higher power felt foreign to him. But as the meeting went on, something began to shift. Person after person shared their story—stories of struggle, stories of hitting rock bottom, stories of feeling lost and powerless. But they were also stories of hope, of change, of finding peace in sobriety.

One man, a middle-aged factory worker, spoke about the day he had realized he couldn't defeat alcohol on his own. "I was just like you, Andrew," he said, his voice calm but full of emotion. "I thought I could beat this if I tried hard enough. But it wasn't about trying harder. It was about surrendering, about accepting that I needed help, and that's when everything started to change."

Ethan listened intently, his heart pounding in his chest. He had heard people talk about recovery before, but it had never felt like this. These people weren't trying to fix him. They weren't offering a magic solution. They were simply sharing their stories, their experiences, and letting him see that recovery was possible.

As the meeting came to a close, a woman across the circle caught Andrew's eye. She smiled and spoke directly to him. "It's okay if you don't have all the answers right now," she said. "None of us did when we started. Just take it one day at a time. That's all any of us can do."

Ethan felt a lump in his throat. For the first time in years, he didn't feel alone. He didn't feel judged. He felt a sense of community, of shared struggle, of people who understood the battle he was fighting because they had fought it too.

After the meeting, Bill turned to him. "What do you think?"

Ethan took a deep breath. "I think... I think I'm willing to give this a chance. I don't know if I understand it all yet, but I'm ready to try."

Bill nodded, his eyes filled with encouragement. "That's all you need, Andrew. Just a willingness to try."

In the days that followed, Ethan continued attending meetings, slowly beginning to work through the 12 Steps. He didn't fully grasp the spiritual aspect of A.A. at first, but he didn't need to. The fellowship, the stories, and the sense of belonging began to plant something deeper inside him. For the first time in years, he wasn't fighting this battle alone.

The first steps were small—showing up to meetings, listening, learning. But as Ethan took those steps, something began to shift within him. He was no longer trying to conquer alcohol on his own. He was surrendering to the process, to the idea that he didn't have to have all the answers, that there was a power greater than himself—whether it was the fellowship, the program, or something spiritual—that could help him find the strength he had been searching for.

It wasn't a sudden transformation. It wasn't a lightning bolt of clarity. But day by day, as Ethan worked through the program, he began to feel something he hadn't felt in a long time: hope.

And with that hope came a new kind of strength—one that didn't come from willpower or control, but from surrender.

For the first time in years, Ethan was beginning to believe that maybe, just maybe, he could find his way out of the darkness.

And that, more than anything else, was enough to keep him going.

One day at a time.

Part III: The Journey to Recovery

Chapter 6: Early Days in Sobriety

The first few days of sobriety felt like a blur for Andrew. His body was still recovering from the years of abuse, and the sudden absence of alcohol left him feeling shaky and restless. Mornings were the hardest—waking up without the usual numbing comfort of a drink made him feel raw, exposed to every worry and anxiety he had buried for years. Nights were no better. Sleep was elusive, and when it came, it was fitful, interrupted by vivid dreams of drinking and waking up in a cold sweat.

Cravings hit him in waves, crashing over him without warning. The familiar urge to reach for a drink, to quiet the noise in his mind, was overwhelming at times. He had never realized how deeply ingrained the habit had become until he tried to stop. His hands would shake, his mind would race, and the temptation to just have "one drink" gnawed at him constantly.

The first time the craving hit, Ethan found himself pacing his small apartment, running through the usual excuses in his head: *Just one won't hurt. You've done well for a few days—what's the harm in a single drink?*

But somewhere, deep down, he knew that "just one" would never be enough. It never had been.

Instead of giving in, Ethan grabbed his phone and dialed Bill's number, his sponsor and the man who had brought him to his first A.A. meeting. His voice was shaky when Bill picked up.

"I... I don't know if I can do this," Ethan admitted, the desperation clear in his tone.

"You don't have to do it alone," Bill said calmly. "That's what we're here for. Are you near a meeting? Can you go right now?"

Ethan hesitated but nodded. "Yeah, there's one starting in about an hour."

"Good. Go to the meeting. You'll feel better afterward."

Ethan hung up and forced himself to get dressed, fighting the urge to skip it. But something Bill had said stuck with him: *You don't have to do this alone.* That, more than anything, had become his lifeline in these early days of sobriety. For the first time, Ethan wasn't trying to carry the weight of his addiction by himself. He had a support system now, people who understood the struggle, who didn't judge him but instead offered encouragement and hope.

The meetings became his anchor. Twice a day, sometimes three, Ethan showed up, sometimes exhausted, sometimes anxious, but always leaving with a renewed sense of purpose. The stories shared by others—men and women who had been where he was, facing their own demons—helped him feel less isolated. There were days when the cravings were intense, when the doubts crept in, but every time he left a meeting, he felt a little stronger, a little more capable of facing the day ahead.

One night, after a particularly difficult day, Ethan found himself sitting at the back of the meeting room, his hands clenched in his lap. He hadn't shared much during the meetings so far, still too hesitant to open up fully, but that night something shifted. As the others went around the circle, sharing their stories of struggle and triumph, Ethan realized how much he had in common with them.

When it was his turn to speak, he hesitated, but finally let out a deep breath. "I'm struggling," he admitted. "Some days I feel like I'm going to give in. The cravings are so strong, and I don't know if I can do this forever. It feels… impossible."

There were nods around the room, sympathetic smiles from those who understood exactly what he meant.

"You don't have to think about forever," someone said quietly. "Just today. Focus on today. Tomorrow will take care of itself."

That simple advice—*just today*—became another mantra for Andrew. He had been so focused on the idea of staying sober for the rest of his life that he had overwhelmed himself with the enormity of it. But now, he began to shift his thinking. He didn't need to worry about next week or next year. He just needed to stay sober today. And that, he thought, maybe he could handle.

The spiritual aspect of A.A. was another hurdle. Ethan had always prided himself on being self-reliant, and the idea of turning his life over to a higher power was difficult for him to grasp. During the meetings, people talked about their spiritual awakenings, about how their connection with something greater than themselves had helped them find peace and strength in their recovery. For Andrew, though, it felt distant—something he couldn't quite reach.

In the quiet moments, when he was alone with his thoughts, Ethan found himself questioning what a higher power even meant. He wasn't religious, and the concept of God felt foreign to him. But as he continued attending meetings, he began to see that the "higher power" didn't have to be a traditional religious figure. It could be the fellowship, the sense of community, the simple belief that there was something greater than his addiction, something that could guide him out of the darkness.

One evening, after a meeting, Bill approached him. "I can tell you're struggling with the spiritual side of things," he said, his tone understanding.

Ethan nodded. "I don't know if I believe in all of that," he admitted. "I've never been one for religion."

Bill smiled. "A lot of us felt that way in the beginning. But it doesn't have to be about religion. It's about finding something bigger than yourself to lean on. It could be the fellowship, the love of your family, even the belief that life can get better. It doesn't have to be complicated."

That simple explanation stuck with Andrew. Maybe he didn't have to define his higher power in a traditional sense. Maybe it was enough to trust the process, to believe that something—whatever it was—was guiding him toward recovery.

As the weeks passed, Ethan found himself opening up more to the idea. He didn't have all the answers, but he didn't need them. He began to pray in his own way, quietly asking for strength to get through the day, for the courage to face his addiction without turning back. It wasn't grand or dramatic, but it felt real. And slowly, he began to feel a sense of peace, a sense that maybe there was something beyond his control helping him stay on the path to sobriety.

The early days of sobriety were a rollercoaster for Andrew. There were moments of doubt, moments when the cravings nearly overwhelmed him, but there were also moments of clarity. He learned to lean on his new support system, to trust the fellowship of Alcoholics Anonymous, and to take each day as it came.

He wasn't alone anymore, and that made all the difference.

Through the support of the group, the encouragement of Bill and the other members, and his growing understanding of spirituality, Ethan was beginning to see that recovery wasn't about being perfect. It was about showing up, doing the work, and believing that there was a way out—one day at a time.

And for the first time in years, Ethan was starting to believe that maybe, just maybe, he could stay sober.

Today, at least. And that was enough.

Chapter 7: Building a New Life

As the weeks turned into months, Ethan found himself deep in the work of the 12 Steps. Sobriety, once a distant dream, had become a daily reality. The cravings hadn't disappeared entirely, but they had lessened, replaced by something stronger: a growing sense of purpose and a commitment to rebuilding the life he had nearly destroyed. But as Ethan worked through the steps, he knew that one of the hardest challenges still lay ahead—making amends.

Step Nine of the program loomed large in Andrew's mind: *"Made direct amends to such people wherever possible, except when to do so would injure them or others."* It was a step that required him to confront the past, to face the people he had hurt during his years of drinking, and to take responsibility for the pain he had caused. It terrified him. Admitting his wrongs was one thing, but seeking forgiveness from those he had betrayed felt like a mountain he wasn't sure he could climb.

The first person he needed to face was Emma.

Ethan had barely spoken to his wife since she had left with their children. The last time they had exchanged words, he had been too drunk to remember most of the conversation, but he knew it had ended badly. She had tried to help him for years, and he had repaid her with broken promises and lies. Now, sober for the first time in years, Ethan knew he had to reach out to her. But what would he say? How could he possibly make up for the years of damage?

With Bill's guidance, Ethan took his time preparing for the conversation. He had learned from the program that making amends wasn't just about saying "I'm sorry." It was about taking responsibility, offering genuine remorse, and being willing to make things right—not for his own peace of mind, but for the sake of the people he had hurt.

One evening, he sat down at his kitchen table, his hands trembling slightly as he dialed Emma's number. He wasn't sure if she would even answer, but to his surprise, she picked up after the second ring.

"Hello?" Her voice was cautious, guarded, as if she were expecting bad news.

"Emma, it's Andrew," he said, his voice steady but soft. "I... I've been wanting to talk to you for a while."

There was a long pause on the other end of the line. "What do you want, Andrew?" she asked, her tone neutral, neither angry nor warm.

"I just... I need to apologize," he said. "I know I've hurt you, more than I can ever say. I've made so many mistakes, and I can't take them back. But I want you to know that I'm sober now. I've been working through the program, and part of that is making amends for the things I've done. I'm not asking you to forgive me, but I needed to take responsibility."

Another pause, longer this time. Andrew's heart pounded in his chest, waiting for her response. Finally, Emma sighed. "Andrew, I'm glad to hear that you're getting help. But it's going to take time. You broke my trust, and the kids' trust, too. You need to understand that."

"I do," Ethan said quietly. "I don't expect anything to be fixed overnight. I just want you to know that I'm committed to staying sober, and I'm willing to do whatever it takes to make things right, if you'll let me."

Emma didn't respond right away, but when she spoke again, there was a trace of something softer in her voice. "I'll think about it," she said. "For now, focus on staying sober. That's the most important thing."

Ethan nodded, even though she couldn't see him. "Thank you, Emma. I will."

The conversation ended without fanfare, but as Ethan set the phone down, he felt a weight lift from his shoulders. It wasn't perfect—there was no sudden reconciliation, no immediate forgiveness—but it was a step. And in that step, Ethan found a sense of peace. He had faced his past, at least in part, and taken responsibility. Now, it was up to him to continue walking the path of sobriety, one day at a time.

Making amends with Emma had been the hardest part, but there were others Ethan needed to face as well. His children, who had grown distant and unsure of him over the years, were next. Rebuilding their trust was going to be a long and delicate process, but Ethan was committed to it. He started small, reaching out to them with sincerity, showing up when he said he would, and most importantly, staying sober. Over time, they began to open up again, though cautiously. Ethan understood that it would take time to heal the wounds he had caused, but he was willing to be patient.

With each amends he made, Ethan felt himself growing stronger. The guilt and shame that had weighed him down for so long began to fade, replaced by a sense of clarity and purpose. He wasn't just staying sober for himself—he was staying sober for the people he had hurt, for the family he had nearly lost, for the future he was trying to rebuild.

As the months passed, Andrew's health began to improve. The damage done by years of drinking didn't disappear overnight, but his body responded to the newfound sobriety. His skin cleared, his energy returned, and the constant fog that had once clouded his mind lifted. He started exercising again, taking long walks in the mornings, enjoying the simple act of breathing fresh air without the weight of a hangover dragging him down.

With his physical recovery came a deeper, more profound personal growth. Ethan began to rediscover who he was outside of alcohol. For so long, drinking had been his identity, his coping mechanism, his way of dealing with life. Now, without it, he was forced to confront the world with clear eyes, and in doing so, he started to find joy in the simplicity of sober living. He reconnected with old hobbies, reading books he had neglected for years, taking up cooking, and even spending time in nature, something he hadn't done since his youth.

There was a quiet beauty in this new life, one that Ethan had never expected. Sobriety had given him a second chance—not just at life, but at living fully, without the haze of alcohol clouding everything. He could see things more clearly now, feel emotions more deeply, and appreciate the little moments that had once slipped past him unnoticed.

In the fellowship of Alcoholics Anonymous, Ethan found a new sense of belonging. The meetings remained a cornerstone of his recovery, a place where he could share his struggles and triumphs with others who understood. He began sponsoring newcomers, offering them the same support that Bill had given him in those early days. Helping others, he found, was a key part of his own recovery. It gave him a sense of purpose, a reason to stay committed to the program.

Day by day, Ethan continued to build his new life, brick by brick. It wasn't perfect, and there were still challenges, but for the first time in years, he felt hopeful. He had faced his past, made amends for his mistakes, and found a sense of peace in the present.

And in that peace, he knew that he had finally found something worth holding onto.

Sober. One day at a time.

Part IV: A Life of Service

Chapter 8: Sponsorship and Service

As Ethan C.'s days of sobriety turned into months, and months into years, his life slowly transformed in ways he hadn't anticipated. The more time he spent in recovery, the more he realized that his journey wasn't just about staying sober—it was about finding a deeper purpose in his new life. That purpose, he soon discovered, lay in helping others who were walking the same difficult path he had once navigated.

Early on, Ethan had leaned heavily on his sponsor, Bill, to guide him through the 12 Steps, to listen when the cravings hit, and to remind him that he didn't have to do this alone. Now, as he gained confidence in his sobriety, Bill suggested that Ethan consider taking on a new role in the program: sponsoring others.

At first, Ethan hesitated. He wasn't sure if he was ready to take on the responsibility of guiding someone else through their recovery. He still had moments of doubt, moments when the cravings resurfaced or when life threw unexpected challenges his way. But Bill assured him that sponsorship wasn't about having all the answers. It was about sharing his experience, strength, and hope with those who needed it.

"It's not about being perfect," Bill said one afternoon, as they sat together after a meeting. "It's about being honest. You've made it through some of the hardest parts, and now it's time to give that back. You remember what it was like in the beginning—how much you needed someone to show you the way. Now, it's your turn."

The idea of giving back, of helping someone the way Bill had helped him, resonated with Andrew. He had come to realize that the 12 Steps were more than just a guide for personal recovery—they were a blueprint for service. Step 12, in particular, emphasized the importance of carrying the message to other alcoholics. Ethan understood now that his own sobriety wasn't just about keeping himself away from alcohol; it was about helping others find their way, too.

Not long after that conversation, Ethan received a call from a newcomer to the program—Tom, a man who had recently attended his first A.A. meeting. Tom's story was painfully familiar: a high-functioning professional whose drinking had spiraled out of control, leading to the loss of his job, his marriage, and nearly his life. He was overwhelmed, scared, and unsure if he could ever find his way back.

Ethan agreed to meet with him, and as they sat together in a quiet coffee shop, Tom shared his fears, his failures, and his hopes for recovery. Ethan listened patiently, letting Tom get it all out. When it was Andrew's turn to speak, he didn't offer grand advice or quick fixes. Instead, he shared his own story—the struggles, the failures, the moments of doubt. He told Tom about the early days when he thought he wouldn't make it, about the nights when the cravings felt unbearable, and about the way the fellowship of Alcoholics Anonymous had given him the strength to keep going.

"I don't have all the answers," Ethan said quietly. "But what I do know is that you don't have to do this alone. We'll take it one day at a time, and together, we'll get through it."

Tom looked at him, his eyes filled with a mixture of fear and relief. "Do you really think I can do this?"

"I know you can," Ethan replied, his voice steady. "Because I did it. And if I can, so can you."

Sponsorship became a central part of Andrew's life. As he guided Tom and other newcomers through the 12 Steps, he found that helping others not only strengthened their recovery but also deepened his own. Each time he shared his story, each time he listened to someone else's struggles, Ethan was reminded of how far he had come—and how close he had been to losing everything.

The act of giving back brought him a sense of fulfillment that he hadn't known before. It wasn't just about staying sober anymore; it was about being of service, about making a difference in the lives of others who were still suffering. He realized that his journey wasn't meant to be walked alone, and neither was anyone else's. The fellowship of Alcoholics Anonymous had carried him when he couldn't carry himself, and now it was his turn to help others stand on their own two feet.

Ethan began speaking more regularly at meetings, sharing his experience with larger groups. At first, the idea of public speaking had intimidated him, but the more he spoke, the more he realized how powerful it could be. People needed to hear that recovery was possible, that even at their lowest points, there was a way out. Andrew's story wasn't unique—so many others in the program had experienced similar lows—but his willingness to share it openly and honestly gave others the hope they needed to keep going.

One evening, after speaking at a particularly emotional meeting, a woman approached him in tears. She had been struggling with her sobriety, unsure if she could keep going, but hearing Andrew's story had given her the strength to hold on for one more day.

"Thank you," she whispered. "I didn't think anyone could understand what I've been through. But you do."

Ethan smiled gently, nodding. "We're all in this together," he said. "Just keep showing up. You're not alone."

As Ethan became more involved in the A.A. community, he found that service wasn't just a part of his recovery—it was the key to maintaining it. The more he gave of himself, the more he received in return. His life, once dominated by alcohol and isolation, was now filled with connection, purpose, and meaning. He had rebuilt his relationships with his family, reestablished trust with Emma and his children, and forged deep bonds with the men and women in the fellowship who had become like a second family.

Through service, Ethan discovered a profound truth: sobriety wasn't just about abstaining from alcohol. It was about living a life of integrity, compassion, and connection. It was about being present for others, about showing up even when it was hard, and about giving back what had been so freely given to him.

As he looked back on his journey, Ethan realized that his darkest days had led him to something far greater than he could have ever imagined. By surrendering to the program, by leaning on the fellowship, and by dedicating himself to the service of others, he had not only saved his own life but had also become a beacon of hope for those still struggling.

In the quiet moments, when Ethan reflected on the years he had spent lost in addiction, he no longer felt shame or regret. Instead, he felt gratitude—for the people who had helped him, for the program that had guided him, and for the opportunity to help others find their way.

And as he continued to sponsor newcomers, to speak at meetings, and to spread the message of recovery, Ethan knew that this was his life's work: to serve, to give back, and to carry the message that had once saved him.

Because in helping others, he had found the truest path to his own healing.

One day at a time.

Chapter 9: A Full Circle

As Ethan C. sat quietly in the back of the familiar meeting room, the low hum of conversation and the soft clinking of coffee cups filled the air around him. It was a place that had become like a second home, a sanctuary of sorts. The room was filled with familiar faces, some new and some weathered by time, all of them bound together by a shared journey. For a moment, Ethan allowed himself to simply observe, to take it all in—the laughter, the quiet words of encouragement, the tears of someone just starting their path to sobriety.

It was hard to believe how much had changed since that fateful day in the hospital. Ethan could still remember the feeling of hopelessness that had washed over him, the certainty that he was beyond saving. He had been broken, physically and emotionally, his life in shambles. Alcohol had stripped him of everything he once held dear—his family, his career, his self-respect. Yet here he was, years later, a man transformed not by his own strength, but by the grace of the program and the fellowship that had lifted him up when he couldn't lift himself.

Sobriety had not come easily, nor had it come overnight. It had been a journey, one that Ethan had learned to approach one day at a time. Each day was a gift, and each day, Ethan reminded himself that his recovery was something to be nurtured, not taken for granted. He had witnessed too many stories of relapse, too many people who had faltered after years of sobriety because they forgot the simple truth: no matter how much time passed, the battle with addiction never truly ended. Sobriety required vigilance, humility, and a willingness to remain connected to the community that had saved his life.

As Ethan reflected on his journey, he couldn't help but feel humbled by how far he had come. It wasn't just about the absence of alcohol—it was about the life he had rebuilt in its wake. His relationship with Emma, once shattered, had healed over time. They weren't the same couple they had been before, but there was a new sense of respect between them, a quiet understanding that had grown out of the ashes of their past. His children, too, had come back into his life, though it had taken time and patience to rebuild the trust he had lost.

But it wasn't just his family that had been restored. Ethan had found a new purpose in his life, one that extended far beyond his own recovery. Through his work in Alcoholics Anonymous, he had helped countless others find their way, just as Bill had once helped him. He had sponsored men and women who had been on the brink of despair, who had walked into their first meeting with the same fear and uncertainty that he had once felt. And as he watched them grow, watched them take their first steps toward sobriety, he saw the ripple effect of recovery in action.

One of those men, Tom, was sitting in the circle today. Ethan watched as Tom shared his story, his voice steady and clear, a far cry from the broken man Ethan had first met in that coffee shop years ago. Tom had struggled in those early days, but he had persevered, and now, he was sponsoring others, passing on the same message of hope that Ethan had once shared with him. It was a full circle moment, one that filled Ethan with a quiet sense of pride—not for himself, but for the power of the program, for the way recovery had the ability to transform lives.

Over the years, Ethan had seen the ripple effect extend far beyond just the people he had sponsored. The men and women who had found sobriety through A.A. had gone on to rebuild their own lives, to heal their families, to reach out and help others who were still suffering. It was a chain reaction, each act of service sparking another, each person finding hope and passing it on to the next. Ethan knew that his own recovery was just one small part of a much larger tapestry, woven together by the countless stories of those who had walked this path before him.

And yet, as he sat in that room, surrounded by the fellowship that had become his family, Ethan understood something even deeper: his sobriety was not his own achievement. It was a gift, one that had been given to him by those who had come before, and one that he had a responsibility to pass on to others. Every time he shared his story, every time he offered a hand to someone just beginning their journey, he was reminded of the simple truth that had saved his life: *Recovery is possible for anyone who is willing to try.*

There had been a time when Ethan believed there was no hope for him, a time when the darkness of his addiction had seemed insurmountable. But through the grace of Alcoholics Anonymous, through the support of the fellowship, and through his willingness to surrender, Ethan had found a new life—one filled with meaning, connection, and hope.

As the meeting came to a close, the chairperson asked if anyone had any final thoughts to share. Ethan hesitated for a moment, then raised his hand. When he spoke, his voice was calm, steady, and filled with gratitude.

"I just want to say that none of us are here by accident," he began. "We're all part of something bigger, something that has the power to change lives. When I first came to A.A., I didn't believe I could recover. I thought I was beyond saving. But this program, and the people in it, showed me that recovery is possible for anyone who's willing to put in the work, to ask for help, and to take it one day at a time. I'm grateful to be here, and I'm grateful to each of you for being part of my journey. None of us do this alone, and that's the beauty of it."

There were nods and murmurs of agreement around the room, and as Ethan sat back down, he felt a deep sense of peace settle over him. He had come full circle, from the man who had walked into his first meeting scared and broken, to someone who could now offer hope to others.

The meeting ended, and as people began to gather their things, Ethan lingered for a moment, watching as friends greeted one another, shared stories, and made plans to meet up later. It was a scene he had witnessed countless times, but today, it felt different. It felt like a celebration—not of him, but of the power of recovery, of the countless lives that had been changed by the simple act of showing up, of sharing stories, of offering hope.

Ethan smiled to himself as he walked toward the door, knowing that he would return, just as he always did, to continue the work that had become his life's purpose. Sobriety, he understood now, wasn't a destination. It was a journey—one that would continue for the rest of his life.

And that journey, more than anything else, was his legacy of hope.

One day at a time.

Epilogue: A New Life

Ethan C. stood at the edge of a quiet park, watching as the sun dipped below the horizon, casting long shadows across the landscape. The evening air was cool and still, and he found himself reflecting on the path that had brought him here—not just to this moment, but to the life he had rebuilt, the man he had become.

Years ago, when he was at his lowest, Ethan had never imagined that a moment like this was even possible. Back then, his life had been consumed by darkness—alcohol had taken everything from him, leaving behind only regret, shame, and the wreckage of broken relationships. His body was failing, his spirit shattered, and his future seemed destined to be a slow descent into oblivion.

But as he stood here now, sober and at peace, Ethan could see his journey for what it truly was: not just a struggle, but a transformation. The pain he had endured, the mistakes he had made, had become the catalyst for his greatest growth. His lowest point—the moment when he had believed there was no hope left—had become the turning point that had led him to a new life.

He remembered that fateful day in the hospital, when Bill and John had first walked into his room and shared their stories of recovery. He had been skeptical then, unsure if he could ever find his way out of the cycle of addiction. But in that moment of surrender, when he had finally admitted that he couldn't do it alone, something inside him had shifted. It wasn't a dramatic revelation, but it was real—a tiny flicker of hope that had been enough to start him on the path to sobriety.

The years that followed had been filled with challenges, but also with incredible growth. Through the fellowship of Alcoholics Anonymous, Ethan had learned to live one day at a time, to lean on others when the weight of his addiction felt too heavy to bear. He had made amends for the wrongs he had done, rebuilt relationships he once thought were beyond repair, and found a deep sense of purpose in helping others who were struggling, just as he had once struggled.

Ethan glanced around the park, watching as families strolled by, children laughing and playing. It was the simple moments like these that he cherished most now—the ones that felt so ordinary, yet held a quiet beauty he hadn't appreciated in his drinking years. Sobriety had given him more than just a second chance at life; it had given him a new way of seeing the world, a new way of being.

But Ethan also knew that his journey was far from over. Recovery, he had learned, wasn't a destination. It was a lifelong process, one that required daily attention and care. There were still days when the cravings resurfaced, when old habits threatened to pull him back into the abyss. But now, he had the tools to navigate those moments—the fellowship, the meetings, the principles of the 12 Steps that had become a part of his everyday life.

He continued to attend meetings, to sponsor newcomers, to share his story with anyone who needed to hear it. Each time he sat in the circle and listened to others speak, he was reminded of where he had come from, and how far he had traveled. He wasn't perfect, and he never would be. But he was sober, and for that, he was profoundly grateful.

As he thought about the people he had met along the way—the men and women whose lives had been touched by the message of recovery—Ethan realized that this was his legacy. Not the career he had once clung to, not the success he had chased in his younger years, but the hope he had passed on to others. He had seen the ripple effect of recovery, how one person's story could inspire another, how one act of service could set off a chain of healing that extended far beyond himself.

And that, more than anything, gave his life meaning.

Ethan took a deep breath, feeling the cool air fill his lungs. He had no illusions that the road ahead would be easy, but he no longer feared the future. He knew now that as long as he continued to live by the principles of the program, as long as he stayed connected to the fellowship, he would be able to face whatever came his way.

One day at a time. It was more than just a phrase—it was a way of life. A reminder that recovery wasn't about perfection, but about progress. About showing up, doing the work, and trusting that there was always a way forward, even in the darkest of times.

As the last light of the sun disappeared over the horizon, Ethan smiled to himself. He thought about the countless people who were still struggling, who felt as hopeless as he once had, and he wished he could tell each of them the same thing that had saved his life:

There is always hope. No one is beyond help. Recovery is possible for anyone who is willing to try.

Ethan knew this to be true—not because of something he had read or been told, but because he had lived it. He was living proof that no matter how far you've fallen, no matter how deep the darkness, there is always a way out. One day at a time.

And that, he thought as he turned to leave the park, was the greatest gift of all.

The End.

Prologue: The Darkness Before Dawn

Elias M. sat alone in the dimly lit apartment that had become both his sanctuary and his prison. The air was stale, heavy with the scent of forgotten meals and empty bottles. His body ached with the familiar, dull pain that had settled into his bones after years of relentless drinking. His hands trembled as he reached for the glass on the table—his last connection to the world he had once known, the world he had lost.

Once, Elias had been someone. He could hardly remember it now, but there had been a time when his name meant something, when his life was full of promise. He had a successful career as an architect, a loving wife, and a future that seemed bright. But that life had slipped away, slowly at first, and then all at once. Alcohol had taken everything from him—his marriage, his work, his sense of self.

Now, as he sat there in the cold silence, Elias felt the weight of his losses pressing down on him, threatening to suffocate whatever was left inside. His days blurred together, one indistinguishable from the next, and the only constant was the drink that numbed the pain. He had become a ghost of the man he used to be, wandering aimlessly through the ruins of his own life.

Elias' thoughts drifted to the people he had pushed away. He could still see the look of disappointment in his wife's eyes the last time she left their home, the way her shoulders sagged as if she had finally given up. His friends had long since stopped calling, and his colleagues had moved on, leaving him to the empty promises and missed deadlines that had defined his later years.

Yet, even as the despair settled in, something stirred within him. It was faint, barely noticeable, but it was there. A memory, perhaps, or maybe just the echo of something he had once known: the idea that life didn't have to be like this. For a moment, Elias wondered if there was still time—time to change, time to rebuild. But just as quickly as the thought entered his mind, it was drowned out by the familiar need for another drink, for the comfort of oblivion.

It wasn't much, that fleeting moment of hope, but it was enough to plant a seed—a seed that would later grow into something more. As Elias reached for the bottle, he couldn't have known that this tiny flicker, this small glimmer of change, would one day lead him down a path he could hardly imagine.

But for now, the darkness was all-consuming, and Elias had no idea that the light would soon find him.

Part I: The Descent into Addiction

Chapter 1: Early Life and Promise

Elias M. grew up in a small town, the kind of place where everyone knew each other's names, and where dreams seemed both expansive and limited by the confines of their surroundings. His parents, hardworking and hopeful, instilled in him the belief that with enough dedication and effort, he could achieve anything. From a young age, Elias was driven. He was curious, thoughtful, and always a step ahead of his peers, excelling in school and showing a remarkable talent for building and design.

By the time Elias entered high school, his passion for architecture had already taken root. He would spend hours sketching buildings, imagining cityscapes, and studying blueprints. His teachers spoke highly of him, often commenting on his potential, and his parents beamed with pride. College was an inevitable next step, and Elias earned a scholarship to one of the top architecture programs in the country. It felt like the world was opening up for him, a world where his creativity and intelligence would flourish.

In college, Elias thrived. His work was praised by professors, and his designs began winning local competitions. He built connections in the industry, impressing everyone with his drive and vision. Success seemed not just within reach but guaranteed. Yet, in the midst of this ambition and excitement, Elias also discovered something else: alcohol.

It started harmlessly enough—weekend parties with friends, a few drinks after late nights in the studio, or a beer to celebrate the end of a particularly grueling project. Alcohol was a social lubricant, a way to relax and let off steam. It wasn't central to his life, just something on the periphery that made the intense world of architecture a little easier to navigate.

At first, Elias didn't think twice about it. After all, everyone around him drank. It was part of the culture—celebrations, networking events, industry parties, and late-night brainstorming sessions were often fueled by rounds of cocktails and toasts to the future. Elias quickly became known as someone who could both work hard and play hard, always balancing the pressure of his demanding studies with the easygoing nature that alcohol seemed to provide.

As Elias graduated and entered the professional world, his career soared. He joined a prestigious architecture firm in the city, working on high-profile projects that put his name on the map. He was young, successful, and well-respected, with a promising future ahead of him. His work ethic and creativity continued to win him accolades, and clients loved his designs. He had achieved everything he had set out to do as a child, and the future seemed limitless.

But as Elias climbed the professional ladder, alcohol became a more frequent companion. Late-night drinks with clients, celebratory toasts after landing new deals, and drinks to unwind after long days at the office became the norm. What had once been an occasional indulgence had now become part of his routine, seamlessly woven into his daily life.

Elias didn't see a problem. He was excelling in his career, maintaining relationships, and living the life he had always dreamed of. Alcohol was just another element of his success, a reward for all the hard work and long hours. And if the drinks came more often now—if they started earlier and lasted longer—well, wasn't that just part of the job? Part of life?

But beneath the surface, the balance was beginning to shift. While Elias continued to perform well at work, there were small signs that something wasn't quite right. He began missing deadlines here and there, forgetting important meetings, and occasionally snapping at colleagues without reason. His once sharp focus started to blur at the edges, and while no one else seemed to notice, Elias felt it. He brushed it off, convincing himself it was just the pressure of success. After all, he was still winning contracts, still getting promotions, still impressing the right people.

As the years went by, alcohol became more than just a social element. It became a coping mechanism. The stresses of high-level projects, the long hours, and the expectations placed upon him were heavy, and alcohol offered a quick escape from the pressure. A drink after work became two. Two drinks became a bottle shared with colleagues, then bottles emptied alone after everyone else had gone home.

Elias still told himself he had it under control. He was a rising star in his field, with a thriving career and a promising future. But as his reliance on alcohol grew, so did the cracks in the foundation of his life. What had once been a harmless companion was slowly becoming something more—something he couldn't quite define, but something that was beginning to take hold in ways he hadn't anticipated.

The people around him began to notice small changes, but no one said anything. After all, Elias was still successful, still charming at parties, still delivering excellent work when it mattered most. But within himself, he could feel a shift—a creeping sense that maybe, just maybe, alcohol wasn't as harmless as he had once thought.

But Elias pushed those thoughts away. He was young, successful, and living the life he had always dreamed of. He wasn't like the others who couldn't control their drinking. He had everything under control—or so he thought.

As the drinks continued to flow, so did the illusion that everything was fine.

Chapter 2: The Slide into Destruction

As Elias M.'s career continued to climb, so did his dependence on alcohol. What had once been a social indulgence had now become an unshakable part of his life. The drinks that were once reserved for special occasions or celebrations were now an everyday necessity. Every morning, Elias woke up with a hangover, a dull headache that he had come to accept as part of his routine. He drank to get through the workday, to silence the constant hum of anxiety that followed him from project to project.

At first, the changes were subtle, barely noticeable to anyone but Elias himself. He began showing up late to work, excusing it as the result of late nights and long hours. His colleagues, who had once admired his work ethic and attention to detail, started to raise eyebrows at his increasing unreliability. Important emails went unanswered, deadlines slipped by, and projects that once would have been his shining achievements began to fall flat.

Elias convinced himself it was just a phase—a temporary dip in performance caused by the pressures of success. But deep down, he knew better. Alcohol was no longer just a part of his life; it was controlling his life. And as his drinking escalated, so did the consequences.

The first real sign that things were spiraling out of control came in the form of a DUI. It happened late one night after a client dinner, where the drinks had flowed freely and without restraint. Elias had insisted he was fine to drive, brushing off the concerned looks of his colleagues as they watched him fumble with his car keys. But just a few miles from the restaurant, he saw the flashing blue lights in his rearview mirror.

Sitting in the back of the police car, handcuffed and ashamed, Elias felt a wave of panic wash over him. This wasn't supposed to happen to someone like him—someone successful, respected, in control. The arrest was a wake-up call, but not the kind that leads to immediate change. Instead, it filled Elias with deeper shame and self-loathing, emotions that only drove him further into the bottle.

His license was suspended, and for a while, he managed to keep the DUI quiet, telling colleagues and friends that he had chosen to take a break from driving. But the cracks were becoming harder to conceal. His work suffered more with each passing week, and the once-promising architect, who had been seen as a rising star in the industry, was now viewed as unreliable, distracted, and on the verge of losing his edge.

At home, Elias' relationships began to fray. His friends, who had once been frequent companions, noticed the change in him. The light that had once driven his passion for architecture was dimming, replaced by a constant state of agitation and fatigue. His once-strong friendships began to dissolve, not with a bang but with a slow, painful drift. He stopped answering calls, stopped showing up to gatherings, and, in time, his friends stopped asking.

The hardest blow came from Emma, his wife. She had been patient—more patient than Elias deserved. For years, she had stood by him, believing that the man she had married would return, that the alcohol was just a phase, that the Elias she loved was still in there somewhere. But as the drinking worsened, so did his temper. The arguments, which had once been about small things—work stress, financial strain—became full-blown confrontations. Elias would come home late, reeking of alcohol, and Emma would beg him to get help. But each time, her pleas fell on deaf ears.

"I'm fine, Emma. It's just work stress. I'm handling it."

But he wasn't handling it. He was barely holding on.

The final straw came one evening when Elias didn't come home at all. After a particularly heavy night of drinking, he had passed out in his car, too intoxicated to even make it inside. When Emma found him the next morning, slumped over the steering wheel, she didn't cry or scream. She simply packed a bag and left, leaving behind a note that said everything she had tried to say for months:

I can't do this anymore. You need help. I love you, but I can't watch you destroy yourself.

When Elias woke up, hungover and confused, the note felt like a punch to the gut. He stared at it, reading the words over and over, but it didn't seem real. She had left. The one person who had always believed in him, who had stood by him through all the broken promises and missed opportunities, was gone. And for a brief moment, Elias felt the weight of it all—the career he had jeopardized, the friendships he had lost, the marriage he had destroyed.

But instead of facing the truth, Elias turned to the only thing he knew would numb the pain: another drink.

The spiral deepened. He stopped going to work entirely, knowing that his absence was no longer just an inconvenience but a liability. His employer, once patient and supportive, finally let him go. His colleagues, who had once admired his talent, stopped reaching out. Elias was alone, cut off from the world he had worked so hard to build, but instead of pulling himself up, he sank deeper into isolation.

The days blended into nights, and the nights into a fog of alcohol and regret. Elias no longer left his apartment, his world shrinking to the space between his bed and the liquor cabinet. The man who had once been full of ambition and drive was now unrecognizable, a shell of the person he had once been. His physical health deteriorated—his hands shook constantly, his skin grew pale and sallow, and the ache in his liver was a constant reminder of the damage he had done.

Despite it all, Elias couldn't stop. He couldn't stop the drinking, and he couldn't stop the self-destruction. The more he drank, the more isolated he became, and the more isolated he became, the more he drank. It was a vicious cycle, one that he no longer had the strength—or the will—to break.

Elias had once believed he was different, that he could control his drinking, that he could walk the line between success and addiction. But now, sitting in his dark apartment, alone with nothing but his thoughts and a bottle in his hand, he saw the truth: alcohol had taken everything from him.

And still, he drank.

He had become a prisoner of his own addiction, unable to find a way out.

Chapter 3: The Breaking Point

Elias M. had been descending for years, but it wasn't until he found himself lying on the cold tile of his bathroom floor, his body trembling uncontrollably, that he realized he had reached the bottom. His skin was clammy and pale, and a dull ache radiated from his liver, a constant reminder of the years of abuse he had subjected his body to. His head pounded, the familiar throb of a hangover mixed with something deeper, more sinister. He could barely move, his limbs heavy and unresponsive. He had woken up on that bathroom floor more times than he could count, but this time felt different.

This time, it felt like the end.

His chest tightened, and for a moment, Elias wondered if this was it. If his body had finally given up, if the years of drinking had pushed him past the point of no return. His breathing was shallow, each breath a struggle, and he could feel his heart racing in his chest, erratic and wild. Panic seized him, but there was nothing he could do. He was too weak to get up, too weak to call for help. All he could do was lie there, staring at the ceiling, waiting for whatever was coming.

Elias had always believed he had time—time to fix things, time to get his life back on track. But now, as his vision blurred and the sounds of the world around him faded, he realized that time had run out.

For a brief moment, he considered calling someone—anyone—for help. Emma, his estranged wife, came to mind, though he knew she wouldn't answer. She had given up on him long ago, and rightly so. His parents? No, he hadn't spoken to them in months. His friends had all drifted away, tired of his broken promises and constant excuses. There was no one left. No one to save him.

And maybe, Elias thought, he didn't deserve to be saved.

The cold, hard truth hit him then, harder than the physical pain that wracked his body. He had done this to himself. He had driven away the people who loved him, destroyed his career, and abandoned any sense of self-respect he once had. Alcohol had become his only companion, his only comfort, and now it was killing him.

A wave of nausea washed over him, and Elias closed his eyes, willing the feeling to pass. His mind wandered through the wreckage of his life, replaying scenes of failure and regret. He saw Emma's tear-streaked face as she begged him to stop drinking, the way her voice had cracked when she told him she couldn't watch him destroy himself anymore. He saw the look in his boss's eyes the day he was fired, the disappointment etched into every line of his face. He saw himself, younger and full of promise, a man who had dreams, ambition, and hope.

And now, there was nothing left but the bottom of a bottle.

Elias didn't know how long he lay there, drifting in and out of consciousness, but eventually, something shifted. It wasn't the kind of dramatic epiphany he had read about in books or seen in movies. It was quieter, more like a flicker of awareness—the realization that he didn't want to die like this. Not here, alone on the floor, broken and forgotten.

But that awareness was immediately followed by another wave of crushing hopelessness. He had no idea how to stop. He had tried before, countless times, and every attempt had ended in failure. He had promised Emma, his parents, even himself, that he would quit. But every time, the pull of alcohol had been stronger than his resolve. It was as if he were chained to it, unable to break free, no matter how hard he tried.

And now, here he was, at rock bottom.

The faint sound of his phone vibrating somewhere in the distance pulled Elias from his thoughts. He ignored it at first, assuming it was just another bill collector or a voicemail he would never check. But the phone buzzed again, insistent and unrelenting. With a groan, Elias mustered the strength to crawl across the floor, his body protesting with every movement.

He found the phone wedged between the couch cushions in the living room, where it had been left days earlier. His hands trembled as he unlocked the screen, his vision blurry. The name on the caller ID surprised him—*Paul*.

Paul had been a colleague once, back when Elias still had a job. They hadn't spoken in months, not since Elias had spiraled completely out of control. Why would Paul be calling him now? With a shaky breath, Elias answered.

"Elias?" Paul's voice was calm but firm. "I've been thinking about you."

Elias didn't respond at first, too stunned to form words. He hadn't expected anyone to reach out, especially not Paul.

"I know things have been rough for you," Paul continued. "I heard what happened with the job and...everything else. I don't know where you are right now, but if you need help, I'm here."

For a moment, Elias considered hanging up. The shame that had become his constant companion flared up inside him, making him want to retreat back into the darkness he had created for himself. But something in Paul's tone, something genuine and kind, stopped him.

"I...I don't know what to do," Elias admitted, his voice barely a whisper. "I can't stop."

Paul was quiet for a moment, letting the words hang in the air. "You don't have to do this alone," he said finally. "There's a place I know. A group that helped me when I was at my lowest. I think they can help you too."

Elias didn't respond right away. The idea of asking for help, of admitting that he was powerless over alcohol, felt terrifying. But then he thought about the bathroom floor, the empty bottles, the isolation. He thought about the fact that if he didn't do something now, there might not be a next time.

"Okay," Elias whispered, his voice cracking. "I'll try."

And with those words, something shifted inside him. It wasn't hope, not yet, but it was the smallest spark of willingness—the first step on a road he had never expected to take.

Paul gave him the details of a local Alcoholics Anonymous meeting, and for the first time in years, Elias felt the faintest flicker of something resembling hope. It wasn't much, but it was enough to get him off the floor, enough to push him toward a possibility he had long since given up on.

As Elias stood, unsteady on his feet, he looked around the wreckage of his life—empty bottles, unpaid bills, discarded memories—and realized that if he wanted to survive, he had to start rebuilding.

It wasn't going to be easy. He knew that. But for the first time in a long time, Elias was willing to try.

And that was enough. For now, it had to be.

Part II: The Spark of Recovery

Chapter 4: A Chance Encounter

The sunlight filtered through the half-closed blinds of Elias M.'s apartment, casting long shadows on the walls. He sat on the edge of his couch, staring blankly at his phone, his mind replaying the conversation he'd had with Paul just a few days before. It had been the first real conversation he'd had in what felt like months, and the words still echoed in his mind: *"You don't have to do this alone."*

Paul's suggestion of Alcoholics Anonymous had hung over Elias ever since. The idea of walking into a room full of strangers, admitting that he was powerless over alcohol, and asking for help felt impossible. What could a group of people like that really offer him? He wasn't like them, he thought. He didn't need their help. He had gotten himself into this mess, and if there was any way out, surely he had to figure it out on his own.

But deep down, Elias knew that wasn't true. His attempts to quit drinking, to pull himself out of the wreckage, had all failed spectacularly. He had tried cold turkey, tried switching to beer, tried every rationalization he could think of, and nothing had worked. He was spiraling, and the idea of recovery seemed as distant as the man he used to be.

Still, the thought of showing up to an A.A. meeting felt humiliating. Admitting he needed help—that he couldn't beat this on his own—was the last thing Elias wanted to do. It felt like admitting defeat, and Elias wasn't ready for that. He had spent years convincing himself that he was in control, that he could manage his drinking. But now, as he sat in his near-empty apartment, surrounded by the remnants of his shattered life, he knew deep down that control had slipped through his fingers long ago.

The phone buzzed again, and Elias glanced at the screen. It was Paul. He had called several times since their first conversation, checking in, asking if Elias had made any decisions about going to the meeting. Elias had ignored most of the calls, letting them go to voicemail, unwilling to face the reality that someone was offering him a way out—and he was too scared to take it.

But this time, something made him answer.

"Hey, Paul," Elias said, his voice low and tired.

"Elias, I'm glad you picked up," Paul replied, a note of relief in his voice. "I've been thinking about you. How are you holding up?"

Elias rubbed his hand over his face, unsure of how to answer that question. He wasn't holding up—he was barely surviving. "I'm... I'm managing," he said, though even as the words left his mouth, he knew they weren't true.

Paul didn't push, but Elias could feel the concern on the other end of the line. "Look, I know you're going through hell right now," Paul said gently. "But I really think you should give A.A. a shot. Just one meeting. If you don't like it, you don't have to go back. But I've seen it help a lot of people. It helped me."

There was a pause as Elias processed what Paul was saying. He hadn't realized Paul had gone through something similar. Paul had always seemed like he had it all together—successful, confident, in control. The idea that he had once struggled, like Elias was now, felt both surprising and oddly comforting.

"I don't know, man," Elias muttered. "I just... I don't see how sitting in a room full of people and talking about my problems is going to help."

"I get that," Paul replied. "I felt the same way before my first meeting. But it's not about sitting around feeling sorry for ourselves. It's about finding a way to move forward, together. You're not the first person to go through this, and you won't be the last. You don't have to do it alone."

The words hit Elias harder than he expected. For so long, he had been convinced that no one could possibly understand what he was going through. That he was different. But now, hearing Paul talk about his own experience, Elias wondered if maybe he wasn't so different after all.

Still, the idea of walking into that meeting, of facing people who knew the depths of his struggle, terrified him. "I don't know if I can do it," Elias admitted quietly.

"You can," Paul said firmly. "And I'll go with you. There's a meeting tonight at a church nearby. I'll pick you up, and we'll go together. You don't have to say anything. Just listen."

Elias hesitated. His mind raced with excuses—reasons why he shouldn't go, reasons why he didn't need help. But those excuses were growing weaker by the day, and deep down, he knew it. If he didn't do something soon, he wasn't sure how much longer he could hold on.

"Okay," Elias said finally, the word barely above a whisper. "I'll go."

The ride to the meeting was quiet. Paul drove while Elias stared out the window, his stomach twisted into knots. He had no idea what to expect. Would they ask him to share his story? Would they judge him? His mind raced with anxiety, every worst-case scenario flashing through his thoughts.

They pulled up to a small church, its front steps lit by a single streetlight. A handful of people were already milling around outside, some chatting quietly, others making their way inside. Elias' heart pounded in his chest as he watched them, the reality of the situation settling in.

"This is it," Paul said gently. "You don't have to do anything you're not comfortable with. Just listen and see what it's all about."

Elias nodded, but his hands were shaking as he stepped out of the car. Every instinct in his body told him to turn around, to run back to the safety of his apartment, to the bottle that still sat on his kitchen counter. But something deeper, something quieter, pushed him forward.

Inside, the meeting room was simple—folding chairs arranged in a circle, a table with coffee and pamphlets in the corner. The people around him looked normal, ordinary. Some were chatting, some sitting quietly, and no one seemed to pay Elias any special attention.

As the meeting began, Elias felt his nerves start to settle, if only slightly. People shared their stories, each one different but somehow familiar. They talked about the same fears, the same struggles, the same sense of hopelessness that Elias had lived with for years. And yet, there was something else in their voices—something Elias hadn't felt in a long time: hope.

When the meeting ended, Paul turned to Elias. "How do you feel?"

Elias swallowed hard. "I don't know," he said honestly. "But... I think I'll come back."

It wasn't much, but it was a start. And for the first time in what felt like forever, Elias felt the smallest spark of something he hadn't allowed himself to feel in years.

Maybe, just maybe, there was a way out.

And he wasn't alone.

Chapter 5: The First Steps

Elias M. sat quietly in the back row of the church basement, his hands resting on his knees, still unsure if he had made the right decision by coming back. He had attended his first Alcoholics Anonymous meeting only a few days before, and now, as he faced another room of strangers, the familiar feeling of anxiety crept up his spine. But something had compelled him to return—something about the way the people at that first meeting had shared their stories, with an honesty and openness that Elias hadn't expected.

It was that openness that had struck him the most. They didn't speak like people who were defeated, even though many of their lives had been wrecked by alcohol, much like his. Instead, there was a sense of resilience in their words, a quiet strength that Elias couldn't quite grasp but felt drawn to. They spoke about sobriety as if it were a gift, something they cherished. It was foreign to him, but as the meeting progressed, a small part of him wondered if it could be possible for him too.

Tonight's meeting felt different. Maybe it was because he had already broken the ice by attending once, or maybe it was the fact that Paul had introduced him to a few regulars before the meeting began. Either way, Elias didn't feel quite as out of place as he had before. There was a rhythm to the meetings, a comfort in the familiar structure. One by one, people stood up and shared, their voices steady, their stories raw and real.

Elias listened carefully, not ready to share his own story yet, but fully engaged in the experience of hearing others. One man, older and graying at the temples, stood up and began to speak. He introduced himself as Charlie, a long-time member of the group.

"I've been sober for eight years," Charlie began, his voice calm but firm. "And if you'd told me eight years ago that I'd be standing here today, living a life I never thought I deserved, I wouldn't have believed you. But here I am, and let me tell you—it didn't happen overnight. It happened one day at a time. And it happened because of gratitude."

Elias sat up slightly, his attention piqued. Gratitude wasn't something he thought about much. In fact, it was hard to imagine being grateful for anything at this point in his life. He had lost so much—his marriage, his career, his health. The idea of finding gratitude in the midst of all that seemed impossible.

"When I first came to A.A.," Charlie continued, "I didn't understand what gratitude had to do with recovery. I mean, how can you be grateful when your life is in pieces, right? But what I learned, slowly, is that gratitude isn't about pretending everything's perfect. It's about finding the small victories, the things we can appreciate, even when life's a mess. Gratitude is what keeps me sober. It's what keeps me grounded."

Elias shifted uncomfortably in his chair. Gratitude felt like such a distant concept, something reserved for people whose lives were already intact, not for someone like him, who was barely hanging on. And yet, Charlie's words stayed with him. There was something about the way he spoke, with such conviction, that made Elias wonder if gratitude could be part of his recovery too.

The first days of sobriety were brutal. After years of drowning his emotions in alcohol, Elias was suddenly forced to confront them all—raw, unfiltered, and overwhelming. The cravings were intense, clawing at him constantly, whispering that just one drink would make the pain go away. His body ached, his mind raced, and sleep was elusive. There were moments when the urge to drink felt almost unbearable.

But Elias had committed to trying this, and Paul's encouragement helped him stay grounded. Paul had become something of a sponsor to Elias, though they hadn't formally discussed it. He checked in with Elias regularly, reminding him that the road to sobriety wasn't about perfection, but progress. "One day at a time," Paul would say, echoing the words Elias had heard at the meeting. "That's all you have to focus on—just today."

Despite the cravings and the doubt, Elias began to notice small shifts in his day-to-day life. He was more alert in the mornings, no longer waking up with the fog of a hangover clouding his mind. He had more energy, even though his body was still adjusting to life without alcohol. And for the first time in a long time, he was starting to feel... present.

It was in those early days of sobriety that Elias remembered what Charlie had said about gratitude. The idea had stuck with him, though he didn't fully understand how to put it into practice. But one morning, as he stood in his kitchen, staring at a cup of coffee he had actually made instead of stumbling to a café in a drunken haze, Elias felt something unfamiliar—a small spark of appreciation. He was sober. He had made it through another night without drinking. And for that, in that brief moment, he felt a flicker of gratitude.

It was a small victory, but it was a victory nonetheless.

Over the next few days, Elias began to experiment with this idea of gratitude. It wasn't grand or overwhelming. It didn't solve all of his problems or erase the damage alcohol had done to his life. But he started noticing little things—a warm shower, a good meal, a friendly text from Paul. And each time, he made a conscious effort to acknowledge it, even if just to himself.

At meetings, gratitude came up often. People spoke about how being grateful for the small things helped them stay present, helped them resist the urge to drink. Elias wasn't sure if it would work for him, but he was willing to try. He didn't have much left to lose.

One evening, after a particularly difficult day, Elias felt the familiar pull of temptation. The craving for alcohol hit him hard, a deep longing that gripped him as he sat alone in his apartment. His mind raced with excuses—*just one drink wouldn't hurt, just something to take the edge off*. He could feel the weight of the addiction pressing down on him, threatening to break the fragile progress he had made.

But then, out of nowhere, Charlie's words came back to him: *Gratitude is what keeps me sober.*

Elias closed his eyes, taking a deep breath. He thought about the past few days—the small moments of clarity, the mornings where he woke up feeling just a little bit better than the day before. He thought about the fact that, for the first time in years, he was actually trying to do something different. And in that moment, he felt a flicker of gratitude, not for what he had lost, but for what he was trying to regain.

It wasn't much, but it was enough to get him through the night.

And so, Elias continued to take it one day at a time, slowly building his life back piece by piece. The cravings didn't disappear, and the road ahead still seemed daunting, but with each passing day, he found more to be grateful for. The small victories—making it through a meeting, resisting the urge to drink, reaching out to Paul—were starting to add up.

Gratitude wasn't some miraculous cure. It didn't fix everything. But it gave Elias something to hold on to, something to keep him grounded when everything else felt like it was slipping away.

And for the first time in a long time, Elias felt that maybe—just maybe—there was hope.

Chapter 6: Transforming Through Gratitude

In the weeks that followed, Elias M. began to notice something he hadn't expected: sobriety wasn't just about avoiding alcohol. It was about transforming the way he viewed the world—and himself. Early on, his focus had been entirely on what he had lost. His thoughts had been consumed by regret, shame, and the wreckage left behind by years of addiction. But as he continued to attend A.A. meetings and practice the principles he had learned, a slow but significant shift began to occur.

It started with gratitude.

At first, gratitude had felt like a foreign concept to Elias. How could someone be grateful when their life had been shattered? But as the days of sobriety turned into weeks, Elias found himself focusing less on the losses and more on the opportunities in front of him. He was sober—something he hadn't thought possible. His health, though still fragile, was improving. He had a chance to rebuild his life, and as daunting as that felt, it was also a gift. Slowly, Elias realized that focusing on what he still had, rather than what he had lost, was changing the way he viewed his recovery.

One afternoon, after a particularly uplifting A.A. meeting, Paul pulled Elias aside. "I see a change in you," Paul said, smiling. "You're more open, more engaged. You've been coming to meetings regularly, and I can tell you're starting to believe in this process."

Elias hesitated, still not used to accepting praise. "I guess," he replied, unsure. "It's just... I don't know. I'm starting to feel like maybe there's more to this than just staying sober."

"There is," Paul said. "And you're ready for the next step."

"The next step?" Elias asked, uncertain what Paul meant.

"You've been focusing on yourself, which is good. That's where it starts. But the real change comes when you start focusing on others. That's where the gratitude really takes hold. Have you thought about helping someone else in the program? Maybe being there for a newcomer, the way others have been there for you?"

The idea hadn't crossed Elias' mind. He still felt so fragile in his own recovery that the thought of helping someone else seemed impossible. "I don't know, Paul. I'm not sure I'm ready for that. I'm still figuring this out myself."

Paul nodded, understanding. "I get it. But let me tell you something—it doesn't take much. Sometimes, just showing up for someone else is enough. You've made it this far. You have something to offer."

Elias mulled over Paul's words in the days that followed. He had always thought of recovery as a personal journey, something he had to go through alone. But now, as he spent more time in the fellowship, he began to see how much his own healing was connected to the people around him. A.A. wasn't just a support system; it was a community, a place where people helped each other, not because they had all the answers, but because they understood the struggle.

One evening, Elias noticed a newcomer sitting quietly at the back of the room, looking as lost and uncertain as Elias had felt on his first day. The man hadn't shared yet, and it was clear that he was uncomfortable. After the meeting ended, Elias approached him, extending a hand.

"Hey, I'm Elias. I noticed it's your first time here."

The man, who introduced himself as Jack, nodded, his eyes filled with the same mix of fear and hopelessness Elias had carried for so long.

"I remember how hard it was for me to come to my first meeting," Elias said gently. "But I'm glad I did. This place... it's helped me more than I can say. If you ever want to talk, I'm here."

Jack seemed surprised by the offer, but grateful. "Thanks," he said softly. "I don't really know what I'm doing yet, but it helps to know I'm not alone."

Elias smiled. "You're not. None of us are."

It was a small gesture, but as Elias walked away, he felt something stir inside him. For the first time, he realized that helping someone else, even in a small way, lifted his own spirit. It was as if by extending a hand to Jack, he had found another piece of his own recovery.

From that point on, Elias began looking for more ways to help. He volunteered to make coffee at meetings, offered rides to newcomers who needed them, and stayed late to help clean up after the group was finished. These were small actions, but each one felt like a step toward something greater. Elias began to understand that gratitude wasn't just a feeling—it was an action. It was something he could practice every day, not just by appreciating what he had, but by giving back to those who were walking the same path.

Elias also started keeping a gratitude journal. Every night before bed, he wrote down three things he was grateful for. Some days, it was as simple as "I made it through the day without drinking" or "I had a good conversation with Paul." Other days, it was deeper—"I'm starting to forgive myself," or "I'm grateful for the second chance to rebuild my life." This small ritual became a way for Elias to reflect on his progress, to stay grounded in the present, and to focus on the positive, even when things felt overwhelming.

In time, Elias found that gratitude was no longer something he had to force. It came naturally, woven into the fabric of his daily life. He became more mindful of the little victories—waking up sober, feeling physically stronger, reconnecting with his parents. And as he worked through the steps of A.A., especially the step of making amends, he approached those conversations not just out of obligation, but from a place of deep appreciation. He wasn't just apologizing for the harm he had caused; he was acknowledging the opportunity to heal, both himself and the people he had hurt.

As the months passed, Elias realized that his entire outlook had shifted. He no longer viewed himself as a man who had lost everything, but as someone who had been given a chance to rebuild. His sobriety, his health, his relationships—these were all things he had to work for, but they were also gifts, gifts he had learned to appreciate through the practice of gratitude.

There were still hard days, moments when the cravings returned or when the weight of his past felt too heavy. But now, Elias had something to hold on to. He had a community, a purpose, and most of all, he had a new perspective.

He had learned that gratitude wasn't just about being thankful for the good things in life. It was about finding meaning in the struggle, about recognizing that every day sober was a victory, and that even in the darkest moments, there was something to be grateful for.

Elias hadn't just found sobriety. He had found a new way of living.

And for that, he was deeply, profoundly grateful.

Chapter 7: Making Amends and Building a New Life

Making amends was the step that Elias M. had feared the most. Facing the wreckage of his past meant confronting the people he had hurt most deeply—people like Emma, his estranged wife, who had walked out on him after years of broken promises, and his parents, who had watched him spiral into addiction with helplessness and sorrow. Elias had spent so long avoiding these conversations, burying his guilt under layers of alcohol and shame, that the thought of opening those wounds again seemed unbearable.

But as he moved further into his recovery, and as gratitude became a larger part of his daily life, Elias realized that making amends wasn't about dredging up old pain. It was about healing—both for himself and for those he had hurt. It was about taking responsibility for the harm he had caused and acknowledging that he was a different person now, committed to a new way of living. And it was about doing so with humility, not expecting forgiveness, but simply offering sincere apologies and a willingness to make things right.

The first person Elias knew he had to reach out to was Emma. Their marriage had fallen apart slowly, piece by piece, as Elias' drinking worsened. She had been patient for years, trying to help him, urging him to get sober, but eventually, her patience ran out. Elias had pushed her away, time and again, until she had no choice but to leave. When she walked out, Elias had felt anger, then regret, but mostly relief—relief that he didn't have to face the consequences of his actions.

Now, though, Elias saw things differently. He wasn't angry anymore. He was grateful for the time they had shared, grateful that Emma had cared enough to try to help him, even when he had been too lost in his addiction to appreciate it. He knew he couldn't fix what had been broken, but he wanted to offer her the apology she deserved.

He picked up the phone one evening, his hands shaking slightly as he dialed her number. It had been months since they last spoke, and Elias had no idea how she would react to hearing from him.

"Hello?" Emma's voice was cautious, unsure.

"Emma, it's Elias," he said softly, his heart pounding in his chest. "I, uh... I don't want to take up too much of your time, but I've been working through some things. I'm sober now. I've been going to A.A., and one of the steps is making amends. I just... I wanted to apologize. For everything."

There was a long pause on the other end of the line, and Elias wondered if she was going to hang up. But finally, she spoke.

"Elias, I don't know what to say," she said quietly. "I'm glad you're getting help. But you hurt me. A lot. It's going to take time."

"I know," Elias replied, his voice filled with sincerity. "I don't expect forgiveness, Emma. I just needed you to know that I'm truly sorry for the way I treated you. I was so deep in my addiction that I couldn't see what I was doing. But that's not an excuse. You deserved better, and I didn't give that to you."

Another pause, and this time, when Emma spoke, her tone was softer, less guarded. "I appreciate you saying that, Elias. I really do. It means a lot. I hope you can keep moving forward."

They didn't speak for long, but as Elias hung up the phone, he felt an enormous weight lift from his shoulders. He hadn't expected Emma to forgive him right away, but her willingness to listen, her acknowledgement of his apology, was enough for now. It was the first step in repairing what had been broken, and for that, Elias was grateful.

With Emma, the process of rebuilding was slow, but over time, they began to communicate more openly. She saw the changes in him—he was no longer defensive or dismissive, no longer hiding behind alcohol and excuses. Instead, he was present, willing to acknowledge his mistakes, and genuinely committed to making things right. While they didn't get back together, their relationship transformed into one of mutual respect and understanding. The anger and resentment that had once defined their interactions slowly gave way to something more peaceful, more honest.

Next, Elias reached out to his parents. His relationship with them had been strained for years, ever since they had tried to intervene in his drinking and he had pushed them away. He had avoided their calls, refused their help, and isolated himself completely. Now, as he stood on their front porch, preparing to knock on the door, Elias felt a knot of anxiety tighten in his chest.

When his mother opened the door, her eyes widened in surprise. "Elias," she said, her voice filled with a mixture of relief and concern. "It's been so long. Come in."

They sat at the kitchen table, the same table where they had shared countless meals during his childhood, and Elias felt the weight of all the years that had passed between them. He looked at his parents, their faces lined with worry, and for the first time in a long time, he didn't feel defensive. He felt gratitude—gratitude for the love they had always shown him, even when he didn't deserve it.

"I've been going to A.A.," Elias began, his voice steady but emotional. "I'm sober now, and part of the program is making amends. I know I hurt you both, and I'm so sorry for everything I put you through. I was lost, but I'm trying to rebuild my life, and I want to make things right with you."

His mother's eyes filled with tears, and his father, always the quieter one, nodded solemnly. "We've always wanted the best for you, Elias," his father said. "We just wanted you to be okay."

"I know," Elias replied, his voice thick with emotion. "I wasn't ready before, but I am now. I'm sorry it took so long."

In the weeks and months that followed, Elias' relationship with his parents began to heal. They saw the genuine change in him, and their relief was palpable. Slowly, they began to trust him again, and Elias, for the first time in years, felt like part of a family again. Gratitude played a major role in how he communicated with them. He no longer took their love for granted. Instead, he expressed his appreciation openly, making sure they knew how much their support meant to him.

As Elias continued to work through the steps of A.A., he realized that making amends wasn't just about the people in his life—it was about healing his relationship with himself. For years, he had carried shame and self-loathing, numbing himself with alcohol to avoid facing his mistakes. But now, through the practice of gratitude, he was learning to forgive himself, too.

Gratitude had become a daily practice, woven into every aspect of his life. He continued to journal every night, listing the things he was thankful for, big and small. Some days, it was as simple as "I made it through another day sober" or "I had a meaningful conversation with Paul." Other days, it was deeper—"I'm grateful for the opportunity to rebuild my life," or "I'm starting to see my own worth."

With each passing day, Elias grew emotionally and spiritually. He no longer saw gratitude as a fleeting feeling but as a daily action that enriched his life. It was through gratitude that he was able to make amends, not just with the people he had hurt, but with himself. And as his relationships healed, as he grew stronger in his recovery, Elias realized that gratitude had transformed him in ways he never thought possible.

He wasn't just surviving anymore. He was truly living.

And for that, he was endlessly grateful.

Chapter 8: The Ripple Effect

Elias M. had come a long way since the dark days of his addiction. In the quiet reflection of his sobriety, he realized that his recovery journey wasn't just about healing himself—it was about helping others find the same hope and freedom that he had discovered through Alcoholics Anonymous. Gratitude, once a foreign concept to him, had become the cornerstone of his transformation. And now, he was determined to pass that message on to others.

It started with simple conversations after meetings. Elias had begun sharing his story more openly, finding that each time he spoke, it not only helped him process his own journey, but it also resonated with others. There were always newcomers in the group—men and women who walked in with the same fear and uncertainty that Elias had felt on his first day. He could see it in their eyes, the quiet desperation, the uncertainty about whether they could ever escape the grip of alcohol. Elias recognized that look because it had once been his own.

One evening, after a meeting, a young man named Ben approached Elias. He was new to the program, barely a few weeks sober, and the strain of early recovery was evident on his face. His hands trembled slightly as he spoke, his voice laced with both vulnerability and a glimmer of hope.

"I've heard you speak a few times," Ben said, his eyes downcast. "I don't know how you did it, how you turned everything around. I feel like I'm barely holding on."

Elias smiled gently, remembering how overwhelming those first few weeks had been. "It wasn't easy," he said, "but I didn't do it alone. And you don't have to either. Gratitude helped me, more than I ever thought it would. It's not about fixing everything overnight. It's about finding something—anything—to be thankful for, even when it feels impossible."

Ben looked skeptical. "Gratitude? I've lost so much. How can I be grateful when everything's a mess?"

"I used to feel the same way," Elias admitted. "But here's what I learned—gratitude isn't about pretending everything's fine. It's about recognizing the small things that keep you going. I started with just one thing a day—something as simple as 'I'm sober today.' Over time, it grew. It didn't change my circumstances overnight, but it changed how I saw them. It gave me strength to keep going."

Ben nodded slowly, absorbing the words. "Do you really think it can work for me?"

"I know it can," Elias said with certainty. "It worked for me, and I've seen it work for others. Just take it one day at a time."

Elias offered to sponsor Ben, knowing that guiding someone through the program was not only a way to help, but also a way to keep himself accountable. Sponsorship was more than a duty—it was a privilege, a chance to pass on the lessons he had learned. Over the weeks that followed, Elias watched Ben struggle, just as he had, with cravings, self-doubt, and the overwhelming weight of early sobriety. But slowly, Ben began to open up to the idea of gratitude, just as Elias had done before him.

In the months that followed, Elias found himself sponsoring more newcomers, sharing his story at meetings, and volunteering for service roles within the A.A. fellowship. He started speaking at different meetings around the city, not just to talk about his recovery, but to spread the message of how gratitude had transformed his life. Each time he spoke, he emphasized that gratitude wasn't just a tool for staying sober—it was a way to live a fulfilling life, regardless of the circumstances.

"Gratitude isn't just about being thankful for the good times," Elias would say to the group. "It's about finding something to hold on to, even in the darkest moments. When I first came to A.A., I was broken. I had lost everything—my marriage, my career, my sense of self. But what I found through this program, and through the practice of gratitude, was that I still had something worth fighting for. And that something was my future."

His words resonated with the room, and after each meeting, people would approach him, thanking him for sharing his story and for offering hope to those who were just beginning their journey. Elias knew that his story wasn't unique, but that was precisely what made it powerful. It was a reminder that anyone, no matter how far they had fallen, could rise again.

One evening, Elias was sitting in a meeting when he noticed Ben stand up to share. He watched as the young man, who had once been consumed by doubt and fear, spoke with a new sense of confidence.

"I've been sober for six months now," Ben said, his voice steady but emotional. "And I didn't think I'd make it this far. When I first came here, I didn't believe in any of this—gratitude, recovery, any of it. But Elias... he showed me a different way to look at things. He taught me that even on the worst days, there's something to be thankful for. And that's what's kept me going. Today, I'm grateful for this room, for the people here who have helped me, and for the chance to start over."

Elias felt a surge of pride as he listened to Ben's words. He had witnessed firsthand how gratitude had transformed Ben's recovery, just as it had transformed his own. It was a reminder of how powerful the ripple effect of gratitude could be—how one person's healing could inspire another, creating a chain reaction of hope and recovery.

Over time, Elias saw the ripple effect extend even further. The people he had sponsored began sponsoring others, passing on the same message of gratitude that had been given to them. Meetings were filled with stories of how practicing gratitude, even in small ways, had helped people stay sober, rebuild their lives, and find meaning again.

Elias knew that his role as a sponsor and mentor wasn't just about guiding others—it was about reinforcing his own recovery. Each time he helped someone else, he was reminded of the lessons he had learned, the struggles he had overcome, and the gratitude that continued to fuel his journey.

Gratitude had not only transformed his life, but it had also become the foundation of a community of recovery. It was a living, breathing force that extended beyond himself, touching the lives of everyone it encountered. And as Elias sat in those meetings, watching others embrace the same principles that had saved him, he felt a profound sense of fulfillment.

He hadn't just found sobriety. He had found a purpose—one that was rooted in service, connection, and gratitude.

And as he looked around the room, filled with people at different stages of their journey, Elias understood that this was what recovery was truly about: helping each other, lifting each other up, and spreading the message of hope.

Because in the end, gratitude wasn't just something he had learned to practice—it was something he had learned to live.

And that, more than anything, was the greatest gift of all.

Chapter 9: A Life Reborn

Elias M. sat at a park bench, gazing at the setting sun, the sky painted in shades of orange and pink. The air was calm, and a quiet stillness settled around him. It was one of those rare moments of peace that he had come to cherish—moments where the world slowed down, and he could reflect on the journey that had brought him here.

He thought back to the man he had been, the man who had once been lying on his bathroom floor, too weak and lost to imagine a life without alcohol. The man who had been drowning in shame, regret, and hopelessness. That man had felt like there was no way out, that his life was over before it had truly begun.

But now, as he sat in the warm glow of the evening, Elias realized how far he had come. It wasn't just about the years of sobriety he had achieved—though that was something to be proud of—it was about the transformation that had taken place within him. The journey from rock bottom to where he stood now was nothing short of remarkable, and it had been guided by one simple but profound practice: gratitude.

Gratitude had not only kept him sober, but it had become the foundation of his entire life. In the beginning, it had been a lifeline, something to hold on to when everything else felt like it was slipping away. He had learned to be grateful for the small things—each sober day, each conversation with a friend or sponsor, each moment where he felt even a flicker of hope. And over time, those small moments of gratitude had grown into something deeper, something that now touched every aspect of his life.

He had made amends with those he had hurt, rebuilt relationships that once seemed beyond repair, and created new, meaningful connections in the A.A. community. He had found purpose in helping others, in being a mentor and sponsor to those who were just starting their own journey of recovery. And every day, Elias woke up with a renewed sense of appreciation for the life he was living—a life that had once felt so out of reach.

Elias' thoughts drifted back to the countless meetings he had attended over the years. He had seen people come and go, some finding sobriety, others struggling to stay on the path. But no matter where they were in their journey, Elias had learned to approach each person with empathy and understanding. He knew firsthand how difficult it was to climb out of the depths of addiction, and he had learned that everyone's path to recovery was different.

What mattered most, though, was showing up. For himself. For others. For the community that had saved his life. Elias understood now that recovery was not a destination, but an ongoing journey—one that required daily effort, commitment, and gratitude. Sobriety wasn't something that could be achieved and forgotten. It was a gift, one that had to be nurtured, protected, and valued.

And so, Elias continued to attend meetings, even on the days when he didn't feel like it. He continued to sponsor newcomers, sharing his story and guiding them through the steps with patience and care. He continued to practice gratitude, not just in the big moments, but in the everyday details of his life.

Gratitude had become his compass, guiding him through the ups and downs of life. It reminded him to stay present, to appreciate the moments of peace, and to find meaning even in the challenges. When difficult days came—and they still did—Elias no longer saw them as insurmountable obstacles. He saw them as opportunities to grow, to learn, and to deepen his gratitude for the life he had built.

As the sun dipped lower in the sky, Elias thought about the people who had walked this journey with him—Paul, who had taken him to his first meeting and had been a constant source of support; Ben, the young man he had sponsored, who had recently celebrated a year of sobriety; and the countless others whose stories had touched his heart, whose courage had inspired him to keep going.

He realized now that his recovery wasn't just about him. It was about the community that had lifted him up when he couldn't stand on his own. It was about the people who had believed in him when he had lost faith in himself. And it was about the newcomers, the ones just starting out, who looked to him for guidance and hope.

Elias smiled to himself as he thought about how far he had come. He was no longer the broken man who had once believed he was beyond saving. He was someone who had been given a second chance, someone who had learned that life was worth living—and living well.

But most of all, Elias was grateful. Grateful for the people who had helped him, for the lessons he had learned, and for the opportunity to live a life of purpose and meaning. He knew that gratitude would always be at the heart of his recovery, and he was committed to carrying that message forward, to helping others find the same hope and healing that had transformed his own life.

As the sky faded into twilight, Elias stood up from the bench, feeling a deep sense of peace. His journey was far from over, but he was ready for whatever came next. He would continue to walk this path, one day at a time, with gratitude as his guide.

Because for Elias, every day sober was a gift—and that gift was something he would never take for granted.

The End.

Epilogue: The Power of Gratitude

As I look back on my journey, there's one thing I've come to understand above all else: *no one is beyond hope.* When I was at my lowest, I believed I was too far gone, that my life was too broken to be put back together. I thought that the damage I'd done to myself, to my relationships, and to my future was irreparable. But through the grace of Alcoholics Anonymous, and the simple yet profound practice of gratitude, I've learned that even the darkest moments can lead to light.

Gratitude saved my life. It didn't happen overnight, and it didn't take away the challenges I faced. But it did change the way I saw those challenges. It helped me focus on what I still had, rather than what I had lost. It showed me that, even in the hardest times, there was something to hold onto—something to be grateful for. And that small shift in perspective became the foundation for everything that followed.

If there's one message I hope to leave you with, it's this: *gratitude is accessible to everyone, no matter where you are on your journey.* You don't have to wait until things are perfect to start practicing it. In fact, it's often when life feels the hardest that gratitude becomes the most powerful. It doesn't require grand gestures or monumental changes—it starts with the smallest things. The smallest acts of gratitude can lead to the biggest transformations.

So wherever you are, whether you're in recovery or simply navigating life's challenges, I invite you to take a moment today to reflect on something you're grateful for. It doesn't have to be big. Maybe it's the breath you just took. Maybe it's a kind word someone shared with you. Maybe it's the fact that you're still here, still fighting, still showing up for yourself.

Gratitude is more than just a feeling—it's a way of life. It's a daily practice that can change your perspective, heal your relationships, and guide you through even the most difficult moments. And the beautiful thing is, the more you practice it, the more it grows. The more you give thanks for the small things, the more you'll begin to see how much there is to be thankful for.

My life today is a testament to the power of gratitude. It's not perfect, and I still have hard days. But I'm sober, I'm present, and I'm living with a sense of purpose and peace that I never thought was possible. And for that, I will always be grateful.

So as you move forward on your own path, I hope you'll remember this: *gratitude can change everything*. It can transform pain into healing, loss into growth, and hopelessness into hope. No matter where you are or what you're going through, gratitude is a gift that's always available to you.

It's never too late to start. And it's never too small to make a difference.

The power of gratitude is yours. Embrace it, and watch your life transform.

With gratitude,
Elias M.

Silent Battles: The Hidden Struggles of Women

Prologue: The Illusion of Control

My name is Mary L., and for a long time, I had convinced myself that my life was under control. From the outside, everything appeared to be perfectly in place. I had a successful career, lived in a nice apartment, and was known by my friends and colleagues as independent, driven, and capable. People would often remark on how I "had it all together." But what they didn't see, what no one could see, was the storm brewing inside me—the slow but steady erosion of everything I once valued because of one thing: alcohol.

I told myself, over and over again, that drinking was just my way of unwinding, of coping with the pressures of my job and the expectations that came with it. After all, wasn't it normal to have a drink or two after a long day at work? Didn't everyone do it? At first, it seemed innocent enough—glasses of wine at networking events, cocktails at dinner parties, and a drink at the end of the night to take the edge off. But over time, alcohol became more than just a way to relax. It became my crutch.

What I didn't realize, or rather, refused to see, was that alcohol had slowly become the center of my life. It crept into my daily routine until I no longer drank just to celebrate or unwind—I drank to numb the growing emptiness inside me. My friends and family saw the polished version of my life, but behind closed doors, I was losing control.

For years, I denied that I had a problem. I believed I could stop drinking whenever I wanted, that I was strong enough to handle it. I told myself I just needed to get through the stressful periods, and then I would cut back. But that day never came. Each time I tried to quit, I found myself reaching for the bottle again, more convinced than ever that I was still in control.

What I couldn't admit to myself was that I was already lost, deep in denial, unable to see how much I was drowning. Alcohol had become my solution to everything—the stress, the loneliness, the expectations I placed on myself. What I didn't realize was that alcohol had also become my prison, slowly stripping me of the life I once thought I controlled so well.

It took me a long time to see the truth, but when I did, the illusion of control shattered. This is my story—a story of losing everything I thought I was, and finding hope, freedom, and recovery on the other side.

Part I: A Life in Control?

Chapter 1: Early Success

I grew up with the belief that hard work and dedication could lead to anything I wanted. My parents instilled in me the value of independence, of standing on my own two feet, and of excelling in whatever I set my mind to. As a young woman, I thrived on the challenges presented to me—school came easily, and I graduated at the top of my class. College was much the same, and by the time I entered the professional world, I had built a reputation as someone who was driven, ambitious, and fully in control of her life.

In my early twenties, I secured a position at a high-powered company, moving quickly through the ranks. I loved the feeling of success, of being recognized for my abilities. I thrived on the compliments from colleagues and the admiration of my friends. I wore my independence like a badge of honor, proud to be someone who didn't need help, who didn't ask for favors, and who always delivered results.

My days were filled with meetings, projects, and deadlines, while my nights were often spent at networking events or business dinners. It was during these moments of social interaction that alcohol began to enter my life. At first, it was nothing out of the ordinary—a glass of wine at a dinner with colleagues, a cocktail at a celebratory party, or a champagne toast to mark a deal well done. Drinking felt glamorous, a natural part of my success. It was the accessory that went with the image of being a professional woman who had it all together.

There was never a moment when I questioned it. Drinking was just part of the culture, especially in the business world. As a woman trying to prove myself in a male-dominated industry, I felt the pressure to fit in, to be part of the team. Drinks after work were not just a way to relax—they were essential to networking, to building relationships, to showing that I could hold my own in any social setting.

But beyond the professional world, alcohol began to take on a more personal role. I was balancing so many responsibilities—being a career woman, a daughter, a friend—that alcohol became a way to unwind after long days of juggling it all. There was something about coming home and pouring myself a glass of wine that felt earned, a reward for the day's hard work. It never felt excessive or dangerous; it just felt normal.

As a woman, there were unspoken expectations placed on me—expectations that I had internalized without realizing it. I needed to be strong, to be capable, to balance my career with my personal life effortlessly. I needed to excel at work, maintain relationships, and appear poised, all while handling the pressures that came with these roles. Drinking became a way to relieve that pressure, a way to relax and let go of the weight I carried every day.

At first, it all felt harmless. Alcohol was just part of my life, woven into the fabric of my success and social interactions. There were no warning signs, no red flags. I wasn't drinking to escape anything, or so I told myself. I was just doing what everyone else was doing—celebrating my achievements, unwinding after work, and navigating the professional world with a drink in hand. It was glamorous. It was normal.

Or at least, that's what I wanted to believe.

In the early days, I prided myself on how well I balanced it all—work, social life, family, and yes, drinking. There were times when I would have a few too many drinks at a party or an event, but it was never anything that caused concern. I would laugh it off with friends, joking about needing to take it easy next time, and continue on with my life, confident that I was still in control.

But as the years went on, the lines between social drinking and something more began to blur, though I couldn't see it at the time. The pressures in my life didn't ease—they grew. And so did my reliance on alcohol to deal with those pressures. But I didn't notice, because I was still excelling, still managing it all, still wearing the mask of success.

I thought I had everything under control.

But looking back now, I realize that control was slipping away far earlier than I could have ever imagined.

Chapter 2: The Slippery Slope

As the demands of my career intensified, so did the stress, anxiety, and exhaustion that came with it. What had once been a steady climb toward success started to feel more like an uphill battle. The late nights in the office became longer, the expectations higher, and the pressures of maintaining my image—both personally and professionally—began to weigh on me in ways I hadn't anticipated.

And that's when alcohol, once a casual indulgence, became something I relied on more frequently. At first, it was just an extra glass of wine after a particularly long day or a few cocktails at a work event to ease the tension. But slowly, it became a daily habit, something I needed to unwind and quiet the constant buzz of anxiety in my mind.

I told myself it was normal, that everyone I knew did the same thing. We were all professionals juggling a thousand things at once—of course we needed a drink to take the edge off. But gradually, the drink after work turned into two, then three, then an entire bottle. I no longer waited for social occasions to drink. I would come home after a long day, kick off my heels, and pour myself a large glass of wine before I even changed out of my work clothes.

It became my ritual, my escape from the pressure, the way I soothed the endless demands that I felt bearing down on me. I didn't see it as a problem. I wasn't one of those people with a drinking issue. I was just doing what I needed to do to cope. Besides, I was still succeeding at work, still maintaining my friendships and responsibilities. To the outside world, I had it all together. But behind closed doors, the drinking became more and more frequent.

The first signs of trouble appeared gradually, almost imperceptibly at first. I started waking up with more frequent hangovers, though I brushed them off as the price of being a busy professional with an active social life. I'd miss my morning workouts or show up late to meetings, claiming traffic or an urgent call had held me up. My productivity began to slip, though I convinced myself it was just a temporary phase, something that would pass once I got a handle on my workload.

But the truth was, I was starting to rely on alcohol not just to relax, but to function. It became the thing I reached for when I was stressed, anxious, or even just feeling bored. If I had a bad day at work, I'd reach for a drink. If I had a good day, I'd celebrate with one. Every emotion—every situation—became an excuse to drink.

My friendships began to fray, though I couldn't see it at the time. Friends I had known for years stopped inviting me to events, and when we did see each other, they made comments about how much I was drinking. At first, I laughed it off, joking that I could handle it. But deep down, I felt the sting of their words. Still, I convinced myself they were overreacting. I was just having fun, just blowing off steam. They didn't understand the pressure I was under.

But the truth was harder to avoid when it came to work. I began missing deadlines, forgetting important tasks, and losing the sharpness that had once defined me. My boss noticed, and I could feel the tension in our conversations. There were subtle hints that my performance wasn't what it used to be, that I needed to "recommit to my role" and "focus on getting back to where I was." I promised him—and myself—that I would, but the truth was, I didn't know how to. The anxiety I felt about my slipping career only pushed me deeper into my nightly drinking ritual.

There were nights when I'd wake up in the middle of the night, my heart racing, my mind spinning with anxiety about all the things I had failed to do that day. I'd lie awake, staring at the ceiling, wondering how I'd let things get so far out of control. But the next morning, I'd get up, put on my professional face, and do it all over again. And by the end of the day, I'd pour myself another drink, convincing myself that tomorrow would be different.

Externally, the pressure to keep up the image I had built—the independent, successful woman who could handle anything—felt unbearable. I didn't want anyone to know that I was struggling. I had spent so long building this persona that admitting I wasn't coping felt like failure. I had to maintain the illusion that everything was fine, even as I felt like I was drowning inside.

Alcohol became the way I kept up that image. It helped me relax before networking events, where I needed to be charming and sociable. It gave me confidence when I was feeling insecure, masking the anxiety that gnawed at me constantly. It helped me forget, if only for a little while, that I was falling apart.

I told myself that I was still in control, that I could stop drinking whenever I wanted to. But the reality was, alcohol had become my crutch. And deep down, I knew I wasn't just drinking for fun anymore—I was drinking because I didn't know how to face the pressure without it.

As my reliance on alcohol grew, so did the consequences. My emotions became harder to manage. I was irritable, easily angered, and prone to emotional outbursts, which only added to the strain in my personal and professional relationships. But I convinced myself it wasn't the drinking. It was the stress, the demands, the constant juggling of responsibilities.

I told myself that if I could just get through this tough period, things would get better. I would cut back. I would get my life back on track.

But the truth was, I was losing control. And I wasn't ready to face it.

At least, not yet.

Part II: Descent into Addiction

Chapter 3: Losing Control

As the months went on, alcohol became the axis around which my life revolved. What had once been a coping mechanism had now become a necessity. The quiet glass of wine after work turned into multiple drinks, and before long, I was drinking alone, hiding it from everyone. I didn't need a social event or a work function as an excuse anymore—alcohol was now something I needed to get through the day, to silence the growing restlessness inside me.

I started hiding bottles around the house—under the sink, in my closet, anywhere I could reach when the urge struck. I told myself it wasn't a problem because I wasn't drinking at work or stumbling into meetings drunk. But the truth was, I was structuring my life around alcohol, ensuring I always had it nearby. If I had a meeting or a deadline, I'd hold it together long enough to get through the day, knowing that the moment I was done, I'd have a drink in hand within minutes.

The hangovers became more severe. I started waking up with a pounding headache, my body aching, my thoughts foggy from the night before. More often than not, I'd roll over, glance at the clock, and realize I'd already missed an important meeting or was going to be late for work—again. I would scramble to get ready, throwing on the nearest outfit and rushing out the door, telling myself that next time I wouldn't drink so much. Next time I'd be more responsible. But it never changed.

I began missing more and more days at work. I would call in sick, claiming migraines or sudden illnesses, anything to avoid facing my boss or my colleagues. When I did show up, I was always a step behind, trying to catch up on tasks I had forgotten or emails I hadn't responded to. My once-sharp focus was gone, replaced by the constant pull of needing a drink to calm my nerves, to quiet the anxiety that had now become a permanent fixture in my life.

The personal consequences were even more painful. My friendships, which had already started to suffer, now began to crumble. I found myself making excuses to avoid social events, afraid my friends would notice how much I was drinking or see the physical toll it was taking on me. I couldn't hide the bags under my eyes or the weight I had lost from the constant hangovers, but I pretended everything was fine.

At first, my friends tried to help. They reached out, asking if I was okay, if I needed anything. But I pushed them away, embarrassed and ashamed of how far I'd fallen. I stopped returning calls, stopped showing up to gatherings, stopped letting them in. The less they saw of me, the less they could judge. And besides, I convinced myself that they wouldn't understand anyway.

In the moments when I did try to reach out, I couldn't bring myself to admit how bad things had gotten. I'd put on a brave face and say I was just busy with work, that everything was under control, and that I'd see them soon. But it was all a lie. I had isolated myself so thoroughly that I didn't know how to reconnect. I was too ashamed to let them see the real me—the woman who had built a career and life that looked perfect from the outside, but who was now barely holding it together.

The strain also started to show in my family relationships. My parents, who lived in another state, had always been proud of my independence and success, but even they noticed something was off during our phone calls. I'd avoid speaking to them for long, afraid they'd hear the slur in my voice or the exhaustion that weighed me down. When I did visit them, I would hide my drinking, sneaking sips from a bottle I'd brought with me and feigning tiredness when the hangovers caught up with me.

There was a moment, during one of those visits, when my mother looked at me with such concern that I almost broke down right then and there. "Mary, are you sure everything's okay? You seem... different." I remember forcing a smile, saying I was just stressed from work. She didn't push, but I saw the doubt in her eyes.

Physically, I was falling apart. My body was constantly tired, and my immune system seemed weaker than ever. I started having health problems—persistent headaches, stomach issues, and a constant feeling of nausea that would only go away after my first drink of the day. My face looked drawn, my skin pale. And yet, even as I saw the effects that alcohol was having on me, the thought of stopping felt impossible.

I couldn't imagine a life without it. Alcohol had become my crutch, my comfort, the one thing that made everything else seem manageable. When I wasn't drinking, I was thinking about my next drink. It was a constant pull, a need I couldn't shake. The more I drank, the worse I felt, but the worse I felt, the more I needed to drink. It was a vicious cycle, one that I didn't know how to break.

The shame I felt was overwhelming. I couldn't bear to look at myself in the mirror some days, disgusted by the person I had become. How had I gone from the successful, driven woman I once was to this? The woman who missed work, who lied to her friends and family, who couldn't make it through a day without a drink? I hated myself for it, but I didn't know how to stop.

I began to isolate myself even further, avoiding everyone and everything. My apartment became my safe haven, the one place where I didn't have to pretend I had it all together. I could drink in peace, without anyone watching, without anyone judging me. The outside world felt too harsh, too full of reminders of what I had lost.

But as I withdrew deeper into my isolation, I felt lonelier than ever. I was trapped, ashamed of how far I had fallen, but unable to stop. The thought of reaching out for help seemed impossible. How could I admit that I had lost control? How could I face the world after everything I'd hidden?

So I kept drinking. And with every drink, I fell further and further from the woman I had once been.

Chapter 4: Hitting Rock Bottom

The breaking point came on a cold, rainy evening, though the weather hardly mattered. It could have happened on any day, really, because I had been teetering on the edge for months. My life, once so carefully managed, had unraveled entirely, and I was barely holding on.

That evening, I had missed yet another important meeting at work. I was supposed to present a key project, one that could have secured a promotion I had been vying for. But instead of being in the office, I woke up hours later on my couch, still dressed from the night before, an empty bottle on the floor beside me. My head pounded, and the moment I opened my eyes, panic set in.

I scrambled to check my phone—dozens of missed calls, emails, and messages from my boss. The realization that I had missed such an important meeting hit me like a punch to the gut. I had no excuses left, no lies I could tell to cover up the mess I had made. The job I had built my life around, the career that had once given me a sense of identity, was now slipping through my fingers.

I knew what would happen next—another warning, or worse, losing my job entirely. But in that moment, even the fear of losing my career wasn't enough to make me stop. The weight of my failure was suffocating, and instead of facing the consequences, I reached for another drink, hoping to numb the panic, the shame, and the hopelessness.

That night, as the rain tapped against the windows, I sat on the floor of my apartment, completely lost. I had tried to control my drinking for so long, to convince myself that I could manage it, that I wasn't like "those people" who had real drinking problems. But now, the truth was undeniable: I was one of them. And worse, I didn't know how to stop.

My hands shook as I poured another glass of wine, not because I wanted to drink, but because I didn't know how else to cope. I felt trapped in a cycle I couldn't escape, and the weight of my shame pressed down on me. As a woman, I had always believed I had to be strong, in control, capable of handling everything life threw at me. But here I was, a broken shell of the person I had once been.

The isolation I had created for myself felt unbearable. My friends had stopped calling, tired of the excuses and the broken promises. My family was distant, worried but unsure how to help. And at work, I was skating on thin ice, barely able to function. The thought of reaching out to anyone, of admitting how far I had fallen, felt impossible. I believed I was beyond help. That no one could possibly understand the shame I carried as a woman who had let her life spiral out of control.

I sat there, tears streaming down my face, staring at the bottle in my hand. I knew I couldn't keep going like this. My body was giving out, my mind was fractured, and my spirit was shattered. But the idea of stopping felt equally impossible. Alcohol had become my entire life—without it, I didn't know who I was anymore.

The next morning, still dazed and hungover, I received a call that changed everything. It was from Sarah, an old friend I hadn't spoken to in months. She had been one of the few people who had stuck by me in the early days of my drinking, but eventually, even she had distanced herself. I had always assumed she'd given up on me.

"I've been thinking about you," Sarah said softly when I answered the phone. "I know things have been hard. I've heard from a few people that you're struggling, and… well, I just wanted to reach out."

Her words felt like a lifeline. I didn't know how to respond at first, unsure of whether I could trust her kindness or if it was just another opportunity for me to push someone away. But Sarah's voice was calm, steady, without judgment. "I don't know what's going on exactly," she continued, "but I've been there. I know what it's like to feel like you're drowning."

Her admission took me by surprise. I had known Sarah for years, and I had never once thought she struggled with anything like this. She had always seemed so put together. But now, hearing the vulnerability in her voice, I felt a flicker of something I hadn't felt in a long time—hope.

"I went through something similar a few years ago," Sarah said quietly. "I thought I could handle it on my own, too, but I couldn't. I ended up going to Alcoholics Anonymous, and it saved my life. I don't know if you've ever thought about it, but if you want, I could take you to a meeting. No pressure—just... think about it."

A.A. The idea of walking into a room full of strangers, admitting that I was powerless over alcohol, filled me with dread. I didn't belong in a place like that, did I? Wasn't that for people who had lost everything, who were beyond repair? But then again, hadn't I already lost everything that mattered? My job was on the line, my relationships were crumbling, and I had lost all sense of who I was.

"I... I don't know," I stammered, the fear bubbling up in my chest. "I don't think I'm ready for something like that."

"I get it," Sarah replied gently. "I was scared too. But the thing is, you don't have to be ready. You just have to show up. No one's going to judge you. They'll understand, because they've been where you are."

Her words lingered in the air long after we hung up. I spent the rest of the day in a fog, turning the idea of A.A. over in my mind. The thought of admitting I had a problem was terrifying. What if I saw someone I knew? What if people judged me? And worst of all, what if I tried and still couldn't stop?

But at the same time, something inside me was shifting. Maybe it was the hopelessness of knowing I couldn't keep living like this. Maybe it was the memory of Sarah's calm, understanding voice. Or maybe it was just that tiny, flickering hope that things could be different.

That night, for the first time in months, I didn't reach for a drink. Instead, I sat with the discomfort, the anxiety, and the fear, and I wondered if maybe—just maybe—there was a way out.

The next morning, I called Sarah back.

"Okay," I said, my voice shaky but resolute. "I'll go. I'll go to the meeting."

It was the first step on a path I never thought I'd walk. But it was a step toward something I hadn't dared to believe in for a long time: a chance at recovery, and maybe, a chance at hope.

Chapter 6: A New Beginning

The morning after my first A.A. meeting, I felt something I hadn't experienced in a long time—clarity. My body still ached from the years of drinking, and my mind was racing with the usual anxiety, but there was something different about this day. I had taken a step, however small, toward a new life. I wasn't sure what that life looked like yet, but I knew one thing: I wasn't alone anymore.

I went to another meeting that evening, and then another the next day. Soon, attending A.A. became a regular part of my life. I found myself drawn to the women in the group, many of whom had stories so similar to my own. There was something comforting about being surrounded by people who understood the pressures I had been facing for so long—the pressure to be strong, successful, and independent, all while silently struggling with an addiction that I had hidden from the world.

For the first time, I began to let my guard down. In A.A., there was no need to pretend, no need to hide behind the mask of perfection that I had worn for so long. These women had been where I was—some had lost everything, others had nearly destroyed their families and careers—but they were still standing. They were rebuilding their lives, and they were showing me that it was possible to do the same.

One of the most difficult parts of A.A. was working through the 12 Steps. In the beginning, the idea of admitting my wrongs, making amends, and asking for forgiveness felt overwhelming. I had spent so many years avoiding my mistakes, hiding from the shame I carried, that the thought of facing them head-on terrified me. But as I began to work through the steps, something unexpected happened—I started to feel lighter.

One of the first steps was admitting my powerlessness over alcohol. This was a concept that had been so foreign to me at first, but the more

I leaned into it, the more freeing it became. I didn't have to control everything. I didn't have to fix myself on my own. Surrendering didn't mean I was weak—it meant I was finally being honest with myself. And in that honesty, I found a sense of peace that had eluded me for years.

As I moved through the steps, I was forced to confront the fears and insecurities that had fueled my drinking for so long. I had always thought that alcohol was a way to relax, to unwind after a stressful day. But the more I explored my past, the more I realized that alcohol had been a way to silence the voice inside me that told me I wasn't enough. I had spent my entire life trying to prove myself—at work, in my relationships, even to my family—and alcohol had been the crutch I used when the weight of those expectations became too heavy.

But now, as I opened up in meetings, shared my story, and listened to the stories of others, I began to see those fears for what they were—self-doubt, insecurity, and the belief that I had to be perfect to be worthy of love and acceptance. And for the first time, I started to let go of those beliefs.

The early days of sobriety were hard. There were moments when I thought I couldn't do it, when the cravings felt unbearable, and the idea of facing life without alcohol seemed impossible. But little by little, things began to change. I started to see small victories, the kinds of things I had once taken for granted but now felt like monumental achievements.

Waking up without a hangover felt like a gift. My mind, once clouded by alcohol, began to clear, and I found myself thinking more sharply at work, able to focus on tasks without the constant fog I had grown so accustomed to. My health started to improve too. I had more energy, my skin looked better, and I no longer felt the constant fatigue that had plagued me during my drinking years.

But perhaps the most important victory came in the form of my relationships. Slowly, I began to rebuild the bridges I had burned during my years of drinking. I reached out to old friends, cautiously at first, unsure of how they would respond. Some were hesitant, wary of letting me back into their lives after so many broken promises, but others welcomed me with open arms. And the more I shared my story, the more I realized how much I had isolated myself—not just physically, but emotionally.

One of the hardest calls I made was to my mother. We hadn't spoken much since my drinking had gotten worse, and I knew she had been worried about me. When I finally picked up the phone, I was nervous, unsure of how to explain everything. But as soon as she answered, her voice filled with relief.

"Mary, I'm so glad you called," she said, her tone warm and full of concern. "How are you? I've been so worried."

"I'm... I'm okay," I said, my voice shaky. "I just wanted to tell you that I've been going to A.A. I'm sober now, and I'm working on getting better."

There was a pause on the other end of the line, and then she said, "I'm so proud of you, honey. I know it hasn't been easy, but I'm so glad you're getting the help you need."

Her words brought tears to my eyes. For so long, I had feared judgment from the people who loved me most, but now I realized that they weren't waiting to condemn me—they were waiting to help me. That conversation was one of the first steps in healing the relationship with my family, a process that would take time but was now possible because I had finally admitted I needed help.

The days turned into weeks, and the weeks into months. I stayed committed to the program, attending meetings regularly, working through the steps, and forming deeper connections with the women in my group. Each day sober was a victory, but it was more than just abstaining from alcohol—it was about rebuilding my life, piece by piece.

I wasn't the same person I had been when I first walked into that meeting. I was stronger now, not because I had found a way to control my drinking, but because I had learned to let go of the need for control. I had found strength in vulnerability, in admitting my flaws, and in accepting the love and support of those around me.

The healing was gradual, but it was real. And for the first time in years, I could see a future—one that wasn't defined by alcohol, but by hope, connection, and a new sense of purpose.

This was my new beginning, and I was ready to embrace it, one day at a time.

Part IV: Building a New Life

Chapter 7: Making Amends

One of the most challenging yet transformative parts of the 12 Steps is making amends. I had spent so much time avoiding the wreckage of my past, trying to forget the people I had hurt, the promises I had broken, and the damage I had caused. But now, as I worked through the steps, it became clear that I couldn't move forward without confronting those things. Making amends wasn't just about apologizing—it was about healing, for myself and for the people I had hurt.

When I first started reaching out to the people in my life, I was terrified. How could I explain the way I had treated them? How could I ask for their forgiveness, knowing how much pain I had caused? I wasn't sure if they'd even want to hear from me, let alone forgive me. But part of the process was about humility—approaching each conversation with sincerity, accepting whatever response I received, and being honest about my actions.

The first person I reached out to was my mother. We had always been close before my drinking took over, but over the years, I had pushed her away, lying about my life, making excuses for my behavior, and causing her so much worry. I had already told her about my sobriety in our earlier phone conversation, but this time, I wanted to truly make amends.

I sat with her in her kitchen, my hands shaking slightly as I began to speak. "Mom, I know I've hurt you," I said quietly, my voice heavy with emotion. "I know you've spent so many nights worrying about me, and I'm sorry for all the pain I've caused. I didn't mean to push you away, but I know I did. I was lost, and I wasn't ready to admit it. But I'm trying now. I want to make things right."

My mother's eyes filled with tears as she listened. "Mary, I've always wanted what's best for you," she said gently. "I never stopped loving you, even when things got bad. I'm just so happy that you're getting better."

Her words were a balm to my soul. For so long, I had been afraid to face the people I had hurt, afraid of what they would say. But now, hearing my mother's forgiveness, I realized that making amends wasn't just about apologizing—it was about rebuilding the trust that I had lost, slowly and with care.

As I continued to work through the steps, I reached out to other people I had hurt during my drinking years. Some of the conversations were more difficult than others. Some friends had drifted away from me completely, too hurt by my behavior to trust me again, and I had to accept that. Others were more forgiving, relieved to hear that I was working on myself and willing to rebuild our relationships.

One of the hardest conversations I had was with my boss. I had always prided myself on being a strong, capable woman in the workplace, but my drinking had caused me to miss deadlines, show up late, and neglect my responsibilities. I knew I had let him down, and I wasn't sure how he would respond to my apology.

"I know I haven't been the employee I should have been," I told him in his office one afternoon. "I've been struggling with alcohol, and it affected my work in ways that I'm not proud of. I'm in recovery now, and I'm committed to staying sober. I just wanted to apologize for the way I let things slide and for not being honest with you earlier."

My boss looked at me for a moment, then nodded. "I appreciate your honesty, Mary," he said. "I could tell something was off, but I didn't know what was going on. I'm glad you're taking steps to get better, and I hope we can move forward."

His response was professional, but it was more than I had hoped for. It was a step toward repairing the damage I had done, and I left his office feeling lighter, knowing I had taken responsibility for my actions.

As I made amends with the people in my life, I realized something profound: this process wasn't just about them—it was about me. Each conversation, each apology, was a step toward healing from the inside out. I had spent so many years feeling ashamed of who I had become, drowning in self-loathing, but now, with each amends, I began to rebuild my self-esteem.

I had always thought that apologizing would make me feel weak, but it had the opposite effect. It gave me strength. It showed me that I was capable of owning my mistakes, of facing the consequences of my actions, and of doing the hard work of rebuilding trust. Slowly, I began to forgive myself, something I had never thought possible. I realized that while I couldn't change the past, I could take responsibility for it and move forward with integrity.

A key part of my recovery journey was practicing gratitude. Early in the process, I had been so focused on what I had lost—my relationships, my self-respect, my sense of control. But as I worked through the 12 Steps, I began to shift my perspective. I started practicing daily gratitude, making a conscious effort to appreciate the small victories in my life.

I would write down three things I was grateful for each day. Sometimes it was simple things: "I'm grateful for a clear morning," or "I'm grateful I made it through another day sober." Other times, it was deeper: "I'm grateful for the opportunity to rebuild my life," or "I'm grateful for the second chance my family has given me." This practice became a powerful tool for me, helping me stay grounded in the present and focused on the progress I was making.

As I started to appreciate the small things, I found peace in the parts of life I had once taken for granted—my health, the clarity of my thoughts, the ability to rebuild relationships. Sobriety wasn't just about not drinking anymore; it was about reclaiming my life. I was learning to find joy in simple moments, to appreciate the people who had stood by me, and to embrace the daily opportunity to live with purpose.

With each step I took in recovery, I felt more connected to myself and to the people around me. Making amends was more than just an act of apology—it was a way to rebuild my life from the inside out, to heal old wounds, and to create a future I could be proud of. And through it all, gratitude became my guiding light, reminding me that even in the hardest moments, there was always something to be thankful for.

As I continued to practice gratitude and repair the relationships I had broken, I felt a deep sense of peace that I hadn't experienced in years. I wasn't just surviving anymore—I was truly living, one day at a time.

Chapter 8: A Life of Purpose

As I settled into my sobriety, I realized that my journey was about more than just recovery—it was about helping others who were struggling like I once had. After months of attending meetings and working through the 12 Steps, I felt a calling to give back, to use my experience to support other women navigating the treacherous waters of addiction.

Becoming a sponsor was a natural next step for me. I had witnessed the incredible power of shared stories and support in A.A., and I wanted to be that guiding voice for someone else. I started attending the women's meetings regularly, and soon enough, I found myself paired with a newcomer named Lisa.

From the moment Lisa walked into the meeting, I could see the fear and uncertainty etched on her face. She looked as though she were trying to shrink into her chair, desperately hoping to go unnoticed. I recognized that look all too well—the same one I had worn during my first meeting, filled with doubt and shame. I approached her after the meeting, introducing myself and offering my support.

"Hey, I'm Mary," I said gently. "I've been where you are. If you ever want to talk, I'm here for you."

Over the next few weeks, I met with Lisa regularly. I listened as she shared her struggles, her fears, and the moments of darkness that had led her to A.A. I shared my own story with her, emphasizing that women, too, suffer deeply from addiction. I reminded her that she wasn't alone, that there were countless women who had walked the same path and had emerged stronger on the other side.

I found immense fulfillment in mentoring Lisa. Each time we met, I could see her beginning to open up, her confidence slowly building. As she began to work through the steps, she found her voice, too. The transformation was beautiful to witness, and it reaffirmed my belief that recovery was not just about stopping drinking—it was about healing, rebuilding, and rediscovering oneself.

With each person I helped, I realized that my purpose was becoming clearer. I wanted to spread the message that recovery was not only possible, but it was also a journey worth taking. To do that, I began speaking at meetings and events, sharing my story with others. My goal was to ensure that women knew their struggles with alcoholism were just as valid and serious as men's.

At one particular event, I stood in front of a room filled with women, my heart racing as I prepared to speak. I began by sharing my story—the early success, the slow slide into addiction, and the moment I finally reached out for help. As I spoke, I watched the faces of the women in the room, many nodding along, tears glistening in their eyes as they recognized parts of themselves in my journey.

"I'm here to tell you," I said, my voice steady but filled with emotion, "that recovery is possible. It's not an easy path, and it's not always pretty, but it is so worth it. As women, we face unique challenges and pressures, but we also have the strength to overcome them. You are not alone in this fight."

After I finished, several women approached me, expressing their gratitude for my openness. Some shared their own stories of struggle, their voices trembling as they spoke of their experiences with alcohol. I felt an overwhelming sense of connection and solidarity with them, realizing that our shared experiences were the foundation of our healing.

As I continued to share my story, I began to see the impact it had on others. I was reminded of the importance of community in recovery and how vital it was for women to have a space to express their struggles without shame. I became more involved in organizing women's workshops and discussion groups, aiming to create a safe haven for those seeking support.

Living in gratitude became an essential part of my daily life. I embraced the practice of writing in my gratitude journal each night, noting the small victories that came with each sober day. I was grateful for the clarity of my mind, the joy of reconnection with friends and family, and the strength I found in helping others.

Every time I saw a woman walk into a meeting, unsure and afraid, I felt a renewed sense of purpose. I understood the weight of those moments—the vulnerability, the fear, and the hope that they could find their way to freedom, just as I had. My experiences had shaped me, and now, I was using that knowledge to help others find their path to recovery.

The deeper I delved into my role as a sponsor and mentor, the more I realized how intertwined gratitude and purpose were in my life. Helping others illuminated the way forward for me, reminding me of the resilience and strength we all possess, especially as women. It was about lifting each other up, breaking the stigma surrounding addiction, and embracing the power of community.

In those moments of connection, I felt my own healing solidify. I was no longer just recovering from my past; I was actively shaping a new future, one filled with meaning, support, and love.

As I reflected on my journey, I understood that while the path of recovery was ongoing, I was no longer alone. I had found my voice, my purpose, and a community of incredible women who were just as committed to their recovery as I was. Together, we were building a new life, one rooted in gratitude, connection, and hope.

Epilogue: A Message of Hope

As I sit here reflecting on my journey, I can hardly believe how far I've come. Just a few short years ago, I was a shell of the person I am today, lost in the depths of addiction and drowning in shame. I lived in a fog of denial, believing I was in control, but I was far from it. I had surrendered my life to alcohol, and in doing so, I had lost not just my sense of self, but my connections to the people who mattered most to me.

Today, I stand in a place of sobriety and purpose, filled with gratitude for the path I've traveled. Recovery has been anything but easy, and I know it's a lifelong journey that requires constant commitment and effort. But as I reflect on the transformation I've undergone, I see how every struggle has led to personal growth, resilience, and a deeper understanding of who I truly am.

I've learned that recovery isn't just about avoiding alcohol; it's about healing from within, rebuilding relationships, and finding strength in vulnerability. It's about embracing the power of community and recognizing that I don't have to face this journey alone.

Through my experiences, I've come to understand the importance of breaking the stigma surrounding women and alcoholism. For too long, women have suffered in silence, feeling ashamed and alone in their struggles. I want to remind everyone reading this that our struggles are just as real and painful as anyone else's. Women suffer too, and it's crucial that we acknowledge this truth.

My story is a testament to the fact that recovery is possible for anyone, regardless of how deep their struggles may seem. There is hope, and there is healing. I want to empower other women who might feel trapped in their addiction, who might believe they are beyond help, to take that first step toward recovery. You are not alone, and your story matters.

If you are struggling with addiction, I encourage you to reach out for help. Seek support from those who understand, whether that's through A.A., therapy, or supportive friends and family. No one should have to navigate this journey alone, and asking for help is a sign of strength, not weakness.

There is a better life waiting for you—a life filled with joy, connection, and purpose. Every day is a new opportunity to embrace the possibilities that come with sobriety. Recovery is not just a destination; it's a journey of self-discovery and renewal. You can reclaim your life, just as I did, and find the freedom and peace that come from living authentically.

Remember, no one is beyond hope. Together, we can break the silence, share our stories, and support one another in this journey toward healing. Let's lift each other up, celebrate our victories, and show the world that women's struggles with addiction are valid.

This is not just my message—it's our message. Let's continue to fight for our recovery, for our voices, and for the lives we deserve. The path may be challenging, but with courage, community, and a commitment to gratitude, we can build a brighter future together.

The Southern Saga: Tales of Friendship and Resilience

Part I: Life in the South

Chapter 1: A Proud Heritage

Growing up in the heart of the South, my life was steeped in the rich traditions and values of my family. I was raised in a close-knit community where family gatherings were filled with laughter, music, and food—each event a celebration of our heritage. From a young age, I learned the importance of pride and resilience, lessons imparted through stories passed down from generations. My grandparents had faced hardships, yet they emerged stronger, teaching us to appreciate our roots and the strength of our lineage.

Every Sunday, our family gathered for dinner, a tradition that brought us together around a table laden with Southern delicacies. My mother's cornbread was a staple, and my father would often tell stories from his youth, his voice warm with nostalgia. Alcohol was always present during these gatherings, often in the form of sweet tea spiked with bourbon or a cold beer shared among the men. I remember watching my father and uncles laugh heartily as they passed around a bottle of whiskey, the air thick with camaraderie and the unmistakable scent of Southern comfort.

As I grew older, these early experiences began to shape my perception of alcohol. During holidays and celebrations, it was customary for us to partake in drinks, toasting to family, health, and success. It was all part of the Southern charm—an unspoken rite of passage that signified adulthood. I watched older cousins and family friends raise their glasses, and I couldn't wait for my turn to join them, to be part of the festivities, and to feel the warmth of that social connection.

However, as I started to sample alcohol myself, it became apparent that what was once innocent celebration had deeper implications. My first taste of alcohol came during a family barbecue when I was around sixteen. I remember sneaking a sip of my uncle's beer, the bitter taste surprising me, yet I felt a rush of excitement at being part of the adult world. That moment marked the beginning of my relationship with alcohol—one that would become complicated in the years to come.

As I transitioned into my late teens, I began to see how ingrained alcohol was in our culture. It wasn't just for celebrations; it was a way to unwind, to bond with friends, and to navigate the pressures of life. Southern culture normalized heavy drinking, creating a perception that it was synonymous with enjoyment. Whether it was at college football games, birthday parties, or even simple get-togethers, alcohol was always a centerpiece. I quickly learned to associate socializing with drinking, reinforcing the idea that to have fun, I needed to drink.

But amidst this culture of enjoyment, there was an underlying disconnect. While we celebrated together, no one openly discussed the dangers of drinking or the potential for addiction. As a young adult, I began to notice that many of the adults I looked up to had unhealthy relationships with alcohol. I witnessed friends' parents who relied on it to cope with life's challenges, yet these behaviors were often brushed aside with humor or dismissed as part of the Southern way of life. "It's just how we unwind," they would say, as if that were sufficient justification.

In those formative years, I started to understand that what was celebrated in our gatherings could also lead to darker realities. While we raised our glasses in cheer, the lines between enjoyment and dependency began to blur. I would hear whispers about family members who struggled with their drinking, yet their stories felt like the rare exceptions to the rule. The message I received was clear: alcohol was an integral part of our Southern identity, and any negative consequences were something to be hidden away or dismissed.

As I embraced the culture around me, I was unaware of the seeds that were being planted. My early experiences with alcohol became a foundation for what I thought was normal, shaping my beliefs and behaviors in ways that I would only come to understand later. I was proud of my heritage and the resilience that came with it, yet I was oblivious to the struggles that often lay beneath the surface, hidden by our Southern charm.

In those early years, I felt invincible, believing I could navigate this world of drinking without consequence. But as I would soon learn, that belief was just the beginning of a long and complicated relationship with alcohol—one that would take me far from the pride and resilience my family had instilled in me.

Chapter 2: The Slippery Slope

As I entered my twenties, the carefree days of college began to blend into the reality of adulthood. With graduation came new responsibilities—juggling a full-time job, paying bills, and navigating the expectations of my peers. It was during this transition that I noticed a significant shift in my relationship with alcohol. What had started as social drinking quickly morphed into a dependency I never anticipated.

At first, I relied on alcohol to help me unwind after a long week at work. I'd come home feeling the weight of deadlines and responsibilities pressing down on me, and a cold beer or a glass of wine seemed like the perfect remedy. What I didn't realize was that those initial moments of relief were beginning to carve a deeper groove into my life. I started to seek out opportunities to drink more often—happy hours with coworkers, casual get-togethers with friends, and even quiet nights at home became occasions for pouring a drink.

Soon, it wasn't just about relaxing; it became a way to cope with the stress and emotional pain that came with adult life. The pressures I faced were mounting, and instead of finding healthy outlets, I turned to alcohol as a crutch. Each sip dulled the anxiety that seemed to cling to me, making it easier to navigate the chaos. But with each passing week, I found myself reaching for the bottle more frequently, using it as a way to silence the nagging doubts and fears that plagued me.

The consequences of my growing dependence soon began to surface. I started missing opportunities that would have once excited me. Invitations to events became less frequent as I chose to stay in with a bottle rather than face the world outside. My friends began to notice the changes in me, but I brushed off their concerns with laughter, telling them I was just "taking a break" from the chaos of life. Deep down, I felt the pull of regret, but I pushed it aside, convincing myself that I was still in control.

At work, my performance began to slip. I found myself missing deadlines, arriving late, and struggling to focus during meetings. My once-promising career started to feel like a shadow of its former self, and with every mistake, my confidence waned. My boss noticed my decline and began to express concerns about my work ethic, which only intensified the pressure I felt. The shame of letting everyone down mixed with the anxiety of my job, leading me right back to the bottle for comfort.

Relationships began to strain under the weight of my drinking. Friends who had once been my closest companions started to pull away, weary of my excuses and tired of my erratic behavior. The laughter we shared was replaced by silence, the joy of companionship eclipsed by the weight of my addiction. I would tell myself it was just a phase, that they would come around when they saw I was busy with work. But deep down, I feared that I was pushing them away for good.

Denial became my constant companion. I justified my drinking as part of the Southern lifestyle, a cultural norm that celebrated alcohol as a means of connection and celebration. "Everyone drinks here," I would think. "It's just how we unwind." I convinced myself that I could quit whenever I chose, that my drinking wasn't a problem, just a social habit. I held onto this belief like a life raft, unwilling to admit that I was sinking deeper into the very thing I thought was a casual part of my life.

As the weeks turned into months, the lies I told myself began to pile up. I would go through the motions of work, friendships, and family gatherings, all while cradling my secret—a growing dependency that I refused to acknowledge. The familiar sounds of laughter and clinking glasses at Southern gatherings rang in my ears, a reminder that I was part of something bigger, but I was losing touch with the very essence of those moments.

Despite the mounting evidence of my struggles, I held tightly to the notion that I was fine. I brushed off any comments or concerns, dismissing them as misunderstandings. The weight of denial grew heavier, suffocating me as I clung to the belief that I could manage it all on my own. I had built a life that revolved around alcohol, and the thought of facing the truth felt unbearable.

In those moments, I was standing on a precipice, unable to see the impending fall. My Southern heritage had taught me pride and resilience, but I was losing sight of those values. Instead, I was building a façade of control that was slowly crumbling beneath the weight of my addiction. Little did I know that the real journey was just beginning—one that would force me to confront the demons I had hidden for so long.

Part II: Hitting Rock Bottom

Chapter 3: The Breaking Point

The night began like any other—an after-work gathering with colleagues to celebrate a successful project launch. The atmosphere was lively, filled with laughter and the clinking of glasses. I arrived with a sense of excitement, eager to escape the mounting pressures of my job and enjoy some time with friends. As the drinks flowed, so did the banter, and I lost track of time, caught up in the camaraderie of the moment.

But as the evening wore on, I felt the familiar pull of alcohol, and I quickly slipped past my limits. I had been drinking for hours, yet the idea of stopping never crossed my mind. I convinced myself that I was having fun, that I was the life of the party. The laughter and cheers only fueled my resolve to keep the night going. It was supposed to be a celebration, and I was determined to join in wholeheartedly.

Then came the moment that would change everything. As the night drew to a close, my coworkers began to leave, but I wasn't ready to go home. I stumbled into the parking lot, feeling a mix of euphoria and recklessness. Ignoring the voice in my head that warned me against it, I climbed into my car, determined to drive myself home. It was a decision made in the fog of intoxication, one that I would regret deeply.

I remember the drive being a blur. The streets were quiet, illuminated only by the flickering streetlights. I felt invincible, convinced that I could handle it. But reality came crashing down when the flashing lights of a police cruiser lit up my rearview mirror. Panic surged through me as I pulled over, my heart racing. I knew in that moment that everything was about to change.

The officer approached my window, and the world around me faded away. "Have you been drinking tonight?" he asked, his voice steady and authoritative. I tried to formulate a response, but the words wouldn't come. I felt trapped, caught in a web of my own making.

The breathalyzer test confirmed what I already knew: I was over the legal limit. The officer placed me under arrest, and I felt the weight of my choices crashing down on me. I was handcuffed and escorted to the police car, humiliated and ashamed. The ride to the station felt like a lifetime, each second a reminder of how far I had fallen.

In the aftermath of that night, the consequences hit me hard. I faced charges for driving under the influence, lost my job, and received a barrage of disappointed calls from family and friends who had once looked up to me. The shame was suffocating. I felt as though I had betrayed not only myself but everyone who had supported me throughout my life. The image I had carefully crafted—a successful, strong Southern man—had shattered in an instant.

When I returned home, I was a shell of the person I once was. The familiar walls of my house now felt like a prison, each corner a reminder of my failure. I couldn't bear to face my family or friends, knowing I had let them down. I withdrew further into my isolation, hiding away from the world. The thought of seeking help felt impossible; I believed I was beyond redemption.

In those dark days that followed, I sank deeper into despair. I avoided phone calls, skipped social gatherings, and ignored messages from concerned friends. I believed that my shame would consume me, and I couldn't bear the thought of facing anyone, especially those I had hurt. I told myself that I didn't deserve their support, their understanding, or their love.

Alcohol, once a source of comfort and escape, had turned into a weapon that I wielded against myself. I found solace in drinking alone, drowning my sorrows in a haze of regret and guilt. I would sit in my living room, staring blankly at the walls, feeling like a ghost of my former self. I had lost everything—my job, my friends, and my self-respect. The weight of my decisions crushed me, and I felt utterly hopeless.

It was in this isolation that I began to confront the reality of my situation. I had allowed alcohol to dictate my life, to strip away the relationships and opportunities that had once brought me joy. Each drink was a reminder of my failures, a fleeting escape that left me feeling more trapped than before.

As the days turned into weeks, I knew I had to face the truth. I was at rock bottom, and there was nowhere left to go but up. But the thought of reaching out for help, of admitting my struggles to others, felt like climbing a mountain I wasn't sure I could conquer.

In that moment of darkness, I had a choice to make: continue down this path of destruction or take the first step toward recovery. But the thought of seeking help terrified me. I didn't want to face the judgment or shame that I believed would come with it. I felt like I was alone in my struggle, convinced that no one would understand the unique pressures I faced as a Southern man dealing with addiction.

Little did I know that the path to healing was just beginning, and the first step would require me to confront the very fears that had kept me trapped for so long.

Part III: The Spark of Recovery

Chapter 4: A Glimmer of Hope

The days following my arrest were a blur of shame and introspection. I avoided social interactions, retreating deeper into the cocoon of isolation I had spun for myself. My friends had stopped reaching out, and my family's disappointment loomed heavy in the air. In the midst of this despair, I had all but given up hope that anything could change.

But one evening, as I sat on my porch nursing a drink and staring blankly at the street, a familiar face appeared at the end of the driveway. It was Jake, a friend from high school I hadn't seen in years. He had always been the life of the party, the kind of guy who could make anyone laugh. But as he walked toward me, I could see the weight of life etched into his features. There was a softness in his eyes that hinted at his own struggles, though I didn't know it yet.

"Hey, man," he said, his voice gentle. "Mind if I join you?"

I gestured for him to sit, feeling a mix of curiosity and apprehension. I had avoided talking to anyone, afraid of what they would think of me, but there was something about Jake that felt safe. We fell into an easy conversation about the past, reminiscing about our carefree days, but the lightheartedness of those memories only deepened the shadows of my current situation.

After a while, Jake grew serious. "I heard about what happened," he said quietly. "I just want you to know, I get it. I've been there, too."

His words caught me off guard. I hadn't expected him to know about my struggles, let alone share his own. As he opened up about his battles with alcohol, I listened intently. He told me about the moment he hit rock bottom, how he had found himself in a similar position to mine, lost and unsure of where to turn. And then, in a moment of vulnerability, he suggested something I had never considered.

"You should check out A.A.," he said, his tone earnest. "It saved my life. I know it sounds scary, but it might be exactly what you need right now."

I felt a surge of skepticism wash over me. Alcoholics Anonymous? The thought of walking into a room full of strangers, admitting that I had a problem, felt overwhelming. I pictured judgmental glances and whispers behind my back. Yet, looking at Jake, I saw a man who had faced his demons and come out the other side. Maybe he was right.

After he left, I spent the night tossing and turning, unable to shake the idea of attending a meeting. It was the first glimmer of hope I had felt in ages, but fear gripped me tightly. I felt trapped between wanting to change and the crippling anxiety of facing my truth in front of others.

The next morning, I made a decision. I would go to the meeting. I knew I needed help, and the thought of continuing to hide from my problems felt unbearable. I found the nearest A.A. meeting listed online and marked the time on my calendar.

When the day arrived, I stood outside the meeting hall, my heart racing. The entrance was unassuming, with a simple sign that read "A.A. Meeting Here." I hesitated at the door, doubt flooding my mind. What if no one understood? What if they judged me for my past? I took a deep breath, my palms sweaty, and stepped inside.

The room was modest, filled with folding chairs arranged in a circle. A few people were already seated, chatting quietly. As I walked in, I felt out of place, like a stranger in a foreign land. I scanned the faces around me, looking for any sign of recognition, but I found none.

I took a seat at the back, hoping to blend in and go unnoticed. As the meeting began, a woman introduced herself and shared her story. She spoke about her own struggles with alcohol, detailing the pain and loss she had experienced. With each word, I felt a stirring within me—her experiences resonated in ways I hadn't expected.

As the meeting continued, several other individuals shared their journeys. I listened, enraptured, as their stories unfolded—each one echoing my own in ways I couldn't have anticipated. They talked about the pressures of life, the struggles of being a Southern man, and the cultural expectations that often led to isolation.

In that moment, I began to realize that I was not alone. Here were people who had faced similar battles, who understood the weight of the bottle, the fear of judgment, and the loneliness that often accompanied addiction. Their vulnerability and openness sparked something inside me—a recognition that we were all fighting our own demons together.

By the end of the meeting, I felt a sense of belonging I hadn't anticipated. As people began to share their names and reach out to me, I realized that this was a space of acceptance, not judgment. I left feeling lighter, as if a weight had been lifted from my shoulders. The fears that had once held me captive began to dissipate, replaced by a flicker of hope that maybe I could find a way out of this darkness.

As I stepped back into the sunlight, the world felt a little brighter. I was still scared, still uncertain of what lay ahead, but for the first time in a long time, I felt a glimmer of hope—hope that recovery was possible and that I could reclaim my life.

The journey ahead wouldn't be easy, but I was ready to take that first step.

Chapter 5: Committing to Change

Walking out of that first A.A. meeting, I felt a shift within me—a realization that I could no longer ignore the truth. Alcohol had woven itself into every aspect of my life, dictating my choices and relationships. For the first time, I acknowledged that I was powerless over it. This was a monumental step for me, as someone who had always prided myself on being in control. I felt the weight of that admission settle into my bones, but instead of feeling defeated, I felt a spark of determination.

With that resolve came a commitment to the A.A. program. I started attending meetings regularly, immersing myself in the community and absorbing the stories of others who had walked similar paths. The comfort of shared experiences was profound; I was no longer just an isolated individual battling addiction. I was part of a collective effort, surrounded by people who understood my struggles and offered their support without judgment.

In the coming weeks, I formed connections with several other members, particularly fellow Southerners who shared my cultural background. We bonded over the unique challenges we faced—how societal expectations in the South often glorified drinking and how that culture made it difficult to recognize when things had gone too far. I began to understand that our shared upbringing had both influenced our drinking habits and shaped our journey toward recovery.

During one particular meeting, a man named Roy shared his story. He spoke about his battles with alcoholism, the cultural pressures he faced, and how he felt trapped by the expectations of his peers. His words resonated with me deeply, and afterward, we struck up a conversation. Over time, Roy became a friend and mentor, guiding me through the initial phases of my recovery. We often met for coffee instead of drinks, sharing our victories and challenges in navigating this new life.

The sense of community within A.A. was transformative. For the first time, I felt like I belonged somewhere. Each meeting was a reminder that I wasn't alone in my struggles, and the support from others reinforced my commitment to change. I felt a growing sense of accountability, not only to myself but to my newfound friends.

But as with any journey, there were challenges along the way. The early days of sobriety were fraught with temptations and cravings that tested my resolve. I had to confront the reality of social situations without alcohol, a daunting prospect that often filled me with anxiety. I would find myself at gatherings, surrounded by friends who were drinking, and I'd feel the familiar pang of desire tugging at me.

At first, it felt overwhelming. I would sit there, clutching my soda or water, feeling like an outsider while the laughter and cheers swirled around me. The urge to join in—to lose myself in the warmth of a drink—was strong, and I often had to remind myself of the reasons I was pursuing sobriety. I would mentally replay the moments of despair, the consequences of my actions, and the hope I had found in the program.

I learned to navigate these social situations with newfound strategies. I practiced saying "no" and finding alternative ways to engage in the festivities. I focused on connecting with friends through conversation rather than through alcohol. I started to find joy in being present in the moment, experiencing life without the haze of drinking clouding my perception.

There were setbacks, of course. I remember one particular evening at a friend's birthday party, where the atmosphere was filled with celebration. The music was upbeat, the laughter infectious, and as I watched everyone raise their glasses, the familiar temptation crept in.

For a moment, I felt a wave of longing wash over me, the desire to escape into the comfort of a drink bubbling to the surface. I found myself in the bathroom, taking deep breaths, reminding myself of the progress I had made.

"I can do this," I told myself, staring at my reflection. "I am stronger than this craving."

That night, I left the party early, proud of my decision to prioritize my recovery over the fleeting high of alcohol. Each small victory built my confidence, reinforcing the commitment I had made to myself and to the program.

Through it all, I realized that committing to change was not just about stopping drinking; it was about rebuilding my life in a healthier way. I was learning to embrace the challenges and to see them as opportunities for growth. The role of community became even more essential during these early days, reminding me that I didn't have to face these struggles alone.

As I continued to attend meetings and connect with others, I felt a sense of hope blossoming within me. I was ready to embrace this new chapter of my life, one filled with purpose and connection. Committing to change meant more than just sobriety; it was about rediscovering who I was without the crutch of alcohol and learning to live authentically in the world around me.

With each passing day, I felt stronger and more resolute in my journey toward recovery, ready to take on whatever challenges lay ahead.

Part IV: Building a New Life

Chapter 6: Making Amends

The journey toward recovery is as much about healing relationships as it is about finding sobriety. After months of attending A.A. meetings and working through the program, I began to understand that my past actions had consequences that I could no longer ignore. The relationships I had once cherished had suffered greatly due to my drinking, and it was time for me to take responsibility and make amends.

The first person I reached out to was my mother. We had shared so many good times before my addiction consumed me, but the weight of my choices had strained our bond. I had avoided her for too long, believing that I had disappointed her beyond repair. Picking up the phone, my heart raced as I dialed her number. I was filled with both dread and determination, knowing this conversation could be a crucial step in healing.

"Hey, Mom," I said, my voice wavering slightly. "I know it's been a while, and I want to apologize for everything. I've been going through some changes, and I realize how much I've hurt you."

There was a pause on the other end, and I could hear her breath catch. "Mary, I've missed you," she replied, her voice thick with emotion. "I've been so worried about you."

We talked for hours, and I poured out my heart, acknowledging the pain my actions had caused. I told her how my drinking had spiraled out of control and how much I regretted the distance it had created between us. Her response was filled with compassion; she understood my struggles more than I had realized. Together, we began to rebuild the trust that had been lost, brick by brick.

Next, I turned to my friends—those I had pushed away during my darkest times. I decided to invite a few of them over for dinner. I felt nervous, unsure of how they would react. Would they even want to see me again after everything? But as I prepared for the evening, I reminded myself that this was part of my commitment to change.

When my friends arrived, I greeted them with open arms, a smile on my face. The warmth in the room was palpable, but it was also tinged with awkwardness as we navigated the unspoken history between us. I took a deep breath and addressed the elephant in the room.

"I want to apologize for how I treated you all," I said, my voice steady. "I was lost in my addiction, and I pushed you away when I needed you the most. I regret not being the friend you deserved, and I'm committed to making things right."

Their reactions were mixed—some nodded in understanding, while others looked a bit hesitant. I could see that rebuilding trust would take time. But that night, we laughed, reminisced, and began to reconnect. I shared my journey of recovery, and I could feel their walls slowly coming down. Each moment of laughter, each shared memory, felt like a step closer to mending the fractures in our friendship.

As I moved through the process of making amends, I came to realize that this journey wasn't just about seeking forgiveness from others; it was also about learning to forgive myself. I had carried the burden of shame for far too long, believing that my past mistakes defined me. But the more I spoke about my experiences, the more I understood that acknowledging my mistakes was a powerful step toward healing.

Self-acceptance became a crucial part of my recovery. I began to see that making amends wasn't simply about saying, "I'm sorry." It was about understanding the impact of my actions, taking responsibility for them, and allowing myself the grace to move forward. It was a process of redefining who I was—learning that I could be a person who had made mistakes but was also capable of growth and change.

With each heartfelt apology and each moment of vulnerability, I started to shed the weight of guilt and shame that had clung to me for so long. I learned to recognize that while I couldn't change the past, I had the power to shape my future.

The process of making amends was transformative, not just for my relationships with others, but for my relationship with myself. I felt lighter, more liberated from the chains of my past. I had taken responsibility for my actions, and in doing so, I was slowly beginning to rebuild a sense of self that was rooted in honesty and authenticity.

With every conversation, every attempt to repair the damage, I felt a renewed sense of purpose. I was no longer just a man defined by his mistakes; I was a man on a journey of recovery, determined to create a life filled with meaning, connection, and growth.

As I continued to work through the program, I realized that the act of making amends was not a destination; it was an ongoing process. And as I embraced this journey, I began to understand that healing takes time, patience, and a willingness to be vulnerable. But with each step, I was closer to becoming the person I wanted to be—a person who could face the world with integrity, strength, and compassion.

Chapter 7: Embracing a New Identity

As I embraced my new life in recovery, I began to discover a sense of purpose that I hadn't felt in years. With each passing day, I started to peel back the layers of who I was beneath the weight of addiction. I had spent so much time in the fog of alcohol that I had lost sight of my interests and passions. Now, with a clearer mind, I found myself eager to explore the world around me.

I began to dive into hobbies I had neglected during my drinking years. I had always enjoyed painting, but I hadn't picked up a brush in ages. One afternoon, I dusted off my old easel and set it up in my living room. As I mixed colors on the palette and let the brush glide across the canvas, I felt a rush of creativity. The vibrant colors sprang to life, and for the first time in a long time, I felt a genuine sense of joy and accomplishment. Painting became a therapeutic outlet, a way to express my emotions and connect with myself in a meaningful way.

I also rekindled my love for hiking, a passion I had once shared with friends. I started exploring the beautiful trails around my hometown, immersing myself in nature and appreciating the serenity it brought. Each step on the path felt like a step toward reclaiming my life. The fresh air filled my lungs, invigorating my spirit and reminding me of the beauty in sobriety.

With each new interest, I felt my identity shifting. I was no longer just the man defined by his past mistakes; I was becoming someone who was actively creating a new narrative. As I explored these passions, I also felt a growing desire to give back, to use my experiences to help others who were navigating the same challenges I had faced.

That desire led me to begin sponsoring newcomers in A.A. I vividly remember the first time I met with a new member named Sarah. She was scared, uncertain, and much like I had been, hesitant to open up. As we sat down together for coffee, I shared my story—my struggles, my setbacks, and ultimately, my journey toward recovery. I could see the flicker of hope in her eyes as she began to relate to my experiences.

Being a sponsor brought a new sense of purpose to my life. I found fulfillment in guiding others, supporting them through their struggles, and celebrating their victories—no matter how small. It was incredibly rewarding to witness someone find their footing, to see them begin to believe in themselves. Through these connections, I learned that recovery was not just a personal journey; it was a communal one. We were all in this together, and the strength of our shared experiences only deepened my commitment to sobriety.

Living with gratitude became an essential part of my daily routine. I had started a gratitude journal where I would jot down three things I was thankful for each day. Some days, they were simple—like enjoying a cup of coffee on my porch or the beauty of a sunset. Other days, they were more profound, like reconnecting with a friend or celebrating a milestone in my recovery journey.

Practicing gratitude shifted my perspective. I learned to focus on the positives in my life instead of dwelling on what I had lost. Each entry in my journal served as a reminder of the progress I was making and the relationships I was rebuilding. It helped me appreciate the small victories that often went unnoticed in the rush of everyday life.

The relationships I had once damaged were slowly starting to mend. I reached out to friends and family, spending quality time together and nurturing those connections. Each moment spent with them was a reminder of how far I had come and the love and support that surrounded me. I began to see the beauty in these connections, recognizing how much I had taken for granted during my years of drinking.

Embracing this new identity wasn't always easy. There were moments of temptation and reminders of my past that threatened to pull me back in. But with every challenge, I found strength in the community I had built, the passions I was exploring, and the gratitude I practiced daily.

I learned to stand firm in my recovery, armed with the knowledge that I was not alone. The relationships I fostered, the new interests I pursued, and the act of giving back grounded me in my commitment to sobriety. I was becoming the man I always wanted to be—one who lived authentically, connected to himself and to others, embracing each day as a new opportunity for growth and healing.

As I reflected on this journey, I felt an overwhelming sense of hope and purpose. I was ready to embrace whatever lay ahead, not as a man defined by his past, but as a person committed to living a life of integrity, passion, and gratitude. Each day was a chance to rewrite my story, and I was eager to see what the next chapter would bring.

Epilogue: A Message of Hope

As I sit here reflecting on my journey, I am filled with a profound sense of gratitude and awareness of how far I have come. From the depths of addiction to the heights of recovery, my life has transformed in ways I never thought possible. I remember those dark days, the weight of shame and isolation that pressed down on me, suffocating my spirit and blinding me to the hope that lay ahead. Yet here I am, no longer defined by my past but rather empowered by my experiences.

The journey of recovery is ongoing, a continuous path that requires diligence and commitment. There are days filled with challenges and temptations, moments that test my resolve, but I have learned to navigate them with the support of the community I've built. I realize now that recovery isn't a destination; it's a lifelong journey of self-discovery, healing, and growth. Each day presents new opportunities to embrace life with clarity and purpose, and I am determined to keep moving forward.

One of the most important lessons I have learned throughout this journey is the power of sharing our stories. Alcohol addiction carries a stigma, particularly in the South, where the culture often glamorizes drinking as a way of life. But I have come to understand that silence only perpetuates shame and isolation. By opening up about my struggles, I hope to break that stigma, to show others that it's okay to seek help and that we don't have to suffer in silence.

Empowering others has become a cornerstone of my recovery. I now regularly speak at A.A. meetings and community events, sharing my story to illustrate the realities of addiction and the possibility of redemption. When I see the faces of others in the audience, I am reminded that they, too, are capable of change. My experiences resonate with those who have felt the same despair, and I want them to know they are not alone in their struggles.

To anyone reading this who might be struggling with addiction, I want to extend an invitation to seek help. Recovery is possible, no matter how insurmountable your situation may seem. Reach out to someone—whether it's a friend, family member, or a support group. You deserve a life filled with joy, connection, and purpose, just as much as anyone else. Remember, the first step is often the hardest, but it is also the most important.

You are not beyond hope. You are worthy of love and forgiveness, and there is a community waiting to embrace you. Together, we can lift each other up, break the chains of addiction, and create a world where no one feels the need to suffer in silence.

As I continue on this journey, I hold onto the belief that every day is a chance to rewrite our stories. Let us move forward with courage and resilience, armed with the knowledge that recovery is not only possible—it is a beautiful, transformative journey that brings with it a life rich with possibility.

In the spirit of hope and healing, I encourage you to take that first step. You are not alone, and a brighter future awaits.

Sips Across Europe: A Journey Through Drinking Cultures
Prologue: A Toast to Life

As I sit here with a glass of water in hand, I can't help but reflect on my love affair with alcohol—specifically, how it intertwines with the rich tapestry of European culture. For years, I found myself captivated by the traditions, rituals, and social customs that surround drinking across this diverse continent. Each country tells its own story, blending history, pride, and a sense of community through the shared act of raising a glass.

From the bustling cafés of Paris to the lively beer halls of Munich, I have explored the myriad ways in which Europeans engage with alcohol. My travels took me from the vineyards of Tuscany to the pubs of London, and everywhere I went, I encountered not just the beverages themselves but the lifestyles and values that shaped them. In many ways, drinking was never just about the alcohol; it was about the connection to people, places, and traditions that make life richer.

I remember sitting at a small table in a Parisian bistro, sipping a glass of Bordeaux while watching the world go by. The casual elegance of the moment felt perfect—people chatting animatedly, laughter floating through the air, and the sun casting a golden hue over the city. In that instance, I understood how deeply embedded wine was in the fabric of French life, a companion to food, conversation, and connection.

In Germany, I experienced the exuberance of Oktoberfest, a celebration that turned the streets into a sea of laughter, music, and merriment. The camaraderie among strangers as we raised our steins felt like an unspoken bond, a testament to the joy of shared experiences. The hearty clinking of glasses, the joyous shouts of "Prost!" echoed the importance of togetherness in German culture, where beer is more than a drink—it's a symbol of community.

Yet, amid these vibrant experiences, I began to notice a darker undercurrent. While alcohol often brings people together, it also has the power to isolate and destroy. In the midst of laughter and toasts, I watched as some individuals struggled with their own battles with addiction, their joy overshadowed by dependence. These observations planted a seed of reflection in me—what lies beneath the surface of this celebratory culture?

As I embarked on my journey to understand the cultural contexts of alcohol across Europe, I realized that every country had its own unique relationship with drinking. In the Mediterranean, for example, wine was a staple of daily life, consumed with meals and seen as an essential part of hospitality. In contrast, Scandinavian countries often embraced a more restrained approach, where binge drinking could overshadow the social aspect of alcohol.

In Spain, the tradition of tapas encouraged a more communal and leisurely dining experience, where drinks were paired with food, promoting connection and conversation. Yet, the allure of late-night revelry could lead some down a path of excess, leaving a trail of consequences in its wake. Each cultural norm around drinking came with its own set of challenges and celebrations.

As I navigated through these experiences, my fascination deepened. I wanted to understand not just the joy that comes from a shared drink but also the complexities and nuances that surround alcohol consumption in various cultures. Little did I know that this exploration would ultimately lead me to confront my own relationship with drinking, a journey that would reveal the fine line between enjoyment and dependency.

In this narrative, I invite you to raise a glass with me—not just to celebrate the beauty of European drinking culture, but to explore the intricate and often tumultuous relationship we have with alcohol. Together, let us uncover the stories, the struggles, and the triumphs that shape our understanding of this beloved yet dangerous companion.

Part I: A Cultural Tapestry of Drinking

Chapter 1: The French Connection

France has long been celebrated as a haven for wine lovers, and as I embarked on my journey through this enchanting country, I found myself drawn to the allure of its vineyards and the vibrant café culture of Paris. The French approach to wine is not merely about the drink itself; it's about the experience, the artistry, and the connection to the land and its people.

Exploring France

In the heart of Bordeaux, I wandered through sprawling vineyards, the lush grapevines stretching endlessly toward the horizon. The scent of ripe fruit filled the air, and the sun cast a golden hue over the landscape, creating an idyllic backdrop for a wine-tasting adventure. Here, I learned that wine is more than a beverage; it's a way of life. Each vineyard has its own story, its own unique terroir, and the passion of the winemakers is palpable in every bottle.

The French take great pride in their wine, often seeing it as a reflection of their identity and heritage. Wine is integral to the dining experience, elevating meals from mere sustenance to a celebration of flavor and culture. As I sipped my way through tastings, I discovered how the French pair their wines with local dishes, crafting a culinary symphony that dances on the palate.

Personal Experience

One of my most memorable experiences was at a charming Parisian café tucked away on a quiet street. I ordered a glass of rosé, and as I sat outside, the world unfolded before me. People strolled by, laughter erupted from nearby tables, and the aroma of freshly baked croissants wafted through the air. In that moment, I felt utterly immersed in the essence of French life.

As I observed the couples sharing a bottle of wine, the friends gathered around a table filled with cheese and bread, I realized that for the French, drinking is a ritual that fosters connection. It's about taking time to savor not only the wine but also the moments shared with loved ones.

Later that week, I had the opportunity to visit a vineyard in the Loire Valley, where the owner guided us through the winemaking process. He spoke passionately about the land, the grapes, and the delicate balance required to produce the perfect bottle of wine. I was captivated by his enthusiasm, which brought the wine to life in a way I had never experienced before.

Cultural Significance

Drinking in France is deeply intertwined with culinary traditions and social gatherings. Meals are often leisurely affairs, where wine flows freely and conversation takes center stage. The French take their time at the table, enjoying each course while savoring the nuances of the wine that accompanies it. This practice stands in stark contrast to the hurried pace of dining found in many other cultures, where the focus is often on efficiency rather than enjoyment.

Wine is not merely an accessory to a meal; it is an essential part of the experience. French cuisine and wine complement each other in a harmonious relationship, with chefs meticulously selecting wines to enhance the flavors of their dishes. From pairing robust red wines with hearty coq au vin to enjoying crisp whites with fresh seafood, the marriage of food and wine is an art form that the French have perfected over centuries.

In social settings, wine acts as a bridge between people. It fosters camaraderie and encourages conversation, turning meals into celebrations of life. I witnessed this firsthand at a gathering in the countryside, where friends and family came together to share a long meal. As the sun set, casting a warm glow over the table, laughter and stories flowed as freely as the wine. It was a reminder of the joy that comes from connecting with others over good food and drink.

As I immersed myself in the French drinking culture, I began to appreciate the depth and complexity of their relationship with alcohol. It's a culture that celebrates not just the drink itself but the experiences it fosters and the connections it nurtures. Through wine, the French cultivate a lifestyle that values enjoyment, community, and tradition—a philosophy that resonated deeply with me.

In this chapter of my journey, I learned that drinking in France is a beautiful tapestry woven with history, culture, and human connection. It is a celebration of life's pleasures, where each glass poured is an invitation to slow down, savor the moment, and embrace the richness of experience.

Chapter 2: The German Tradition

Germany's beer culture is a vibrant tapestry woven into the fabric of its social life. Known for its rich brewing heritage, the country takes immense pride in its beer, which is not merely a beverage but a symbol of community and celebration. From the legendary Oktoberfest in Munich to the countless local beer gardens, drinking beer in Germany is steeped in tradition and camaraderie, drawing people together in a way that few other cultures can replicate.

German Beer Culture
Oktoberfest is perhaps the most iconic representation of German beer culture. Each autumn, millions flock to Munich to partake in this world-renowned festival, where massive tents filled with long wooden tables are lined with people clinking steins of beer, singing folk songs, and enjoying hearty traditional food. The festival is a celebration of Bavarian culture, attracting visitors from all over the globe. As I wandered through the colorful grounds, I was struck by the palpable excitement and joy that filled the air.

But Oktoberfest is just the tip of the iceberg. Germany boasts a rich history of brewing that dates back centuries. Each region has its own distinct beer styles, from the crisp and refreshing Hefeweizen of Bavaria to the malty Dunkel of Franconia. This regional diversity is a point of pride for Germans, who often have strong loyalties to their local breweries.

Beer gardens, or Biergärten, are another cornerstone of German drinking culture. These outdoor spaces invite people to relax, socialize, and enjoy a pint under the shade of trees. The atmosphere is casual and welcoming, encouraging conversations among strangers and friends alike. In this communal setting, I found that beer became a conduit for connection, fostering a sense of belonging that resonated deeply with me.

Personal Experience

During my time in Germany, I had the opportunity to attend a local beer festival in a small town nestled in the Bavarian Alps. As I entered the festival grounds, the smell of grilled sausages wafted through the air, mingling with the sound of live music and laughter. Festively adorned tents beckoned me to step inside, and I could see rows of people raising their steins, their faces lit with joy.

With each stein of beer I raised, I felt the spirit of the festival wash over me. The atmosphere was infectious, and I quickly found myself swept up in the celebration. I joined in singing traditional German songs, and the clinking of glasses resonated like a chorus of camaraderie. However, as the night wore on, I felt the familiar tug of temptation pulling me deeper into indulgence.

Navigating the balance between enjoyment and excess became a challenge. Surrounded by friends and fellow revelers, the line between celebrating and overindulging began to blur. I could feel the effects of the beer taking hold, the euphoria mingling with the worry of crossing that invisible line into recklessness. I took a moment to step away from the crowd, leaning against a tree as I gathered my thoughts. I reminded myself of the lessons I had learned in recovery—about moderation, mindfulness, and the importance of being present.

Cultural Insights

Germany's relationship with beer is deeply rooted in its history. The Reinheitsgebot, or Beer Purity Law, established in 1516, dictated that only four ingredients—water, barley, hops, and yeast—could be used in brewing. This law not only ensured quality but also instilled a sense of pride in German brewers, who took their craft seriously.

This historical backdrop shapes how beer is consumed today. Unlike many cultures where alcohol is often associated with reckless abandon, Germans approach beer with a sense of respect and responsibility. Drinking is embedded in social traditions, celebrated during festivals and gatherings but never taken lightly. The emphasis is on enjoying the moment, savoring the flavors, and embracing the community that comes with it.

As I immersed myself in the festival, I saw how the act of drinking beer was not merely about the alcohol; it was about connection, celebration, and heritage. It was a reminder of the importance of balancing enjoyment with mindfulness—an idea that resonated deeply within me.

In that moment, I realized that my experiences in Germany were not just about indulging in beer but about embracing a culture that valued community and tradition. It was a reflection of the journey I was on—a journey of transformation that required both celebration and self-awareness.

As the night drew to a close, I raised my stein one last time, feeling grateful for the moments shared, the connections forged, and the lessons learned. My experiences at the festival served as a poignant reminder of the importance of savoring life's pleasures while maintaining a sense of balance. In that spirit, I left the festival with a renewed sense of purpose, eager to continue exploring the rich tapestry of drinking culture throughout Europe, one experience at a time.

Chapter 3: The British Pub Scene

In Britain, the pub is more than just a place to grab a drink; it is a cornerstone of social life and community. These establishments serve as gathering places where friends and families come together, where conversations flow as freely as the beer. Pubs embody a rich cultural heritage, reflecting the heart and soul of British society.

The Role of Pubs

As I navigated the streets of London, I was drawn to the warmth and charm of its pubs. With their welcoming façades, wooden beams, and the inviting glow of low-hanging lights, pubs beckoned passersby to step inside and experience a slice of British life. Each pub has its own unique character, from historic establishments that date back centuries to modern craft beer bars that showcase innovative brews.

Pubs serve as social hubs, fostering connections among locals and visitors alike. They offer a sense of belonging, a place where regulars gather to unwind after a long day, catch up on the latest gossip, or engage in spirited discussions about football or politics. The camaraderie found in these spaces is palpable, as laughter and animated conversations fill the air, creating an atmosphere that feels alive with energy.

One evening, I found myself in a cozy pub in the heart of Soho, surrounded by the hum of conversation and the clinking of glasses. The smell of hearty pub fare wafted through the air, and I could see patrons enjoying plates of fish and chips, bangers and mash, and other classic British dishes. I settled onto a barstool, eager to sample the local ales. The bartender, a friendly chap with a thick accent, guided me through the selection of beers, each one telling a story of its own.

Personal Experience

As I sipped on a crisp pint of pale ale, I marveled at the variety of flavors and styles available. Each beer seemed to capture the essence of the region it came from. I struck up a conversation with a couple seated nearby, who eagerly shared their favorites and recommended hidden gems across the city.

The night unfolded with laughter and new friendships, the conversation flowing seamlessly between the rich history of the pub and the latest news. It struck me how the pub environment facilitated connections—strangers became friends over shared pints and stories. As the evening wore on, I found myself joining in a game of darts, laughing alongside my new companions as we cheered each other on.

In that moment, I realized that the British pub was more than just a venue for drinks; it was a vital part of the social fabric that knitted the community together. The act of gathering in a pub had the power to transcend barriers, bringing people from all walks of life together to celebrate, commiserate, and connect.

Cultural Commentary

Historically, pubs have played a significant role in British culture, evolving from simple alehouses in medieval times to the multifaceted establishments we see today. They have been places of refuge, social interaction, and even political discourse. In the 19th century, pubs served as venues for organizing labor movements and social change, highlighting their importance in shaping British society.

The evolution of pub culture is also tied to the rise of the working class. As the Industrial Revolution transformed urban life, pubs became essential meeting points for workers seeking camaraderie after long hours in factories. The concept of the "public house" emerged, signifying a space open to all, where everyone could gather and partake in the joy of community.

However, in recent years, the pub scene has faced challenges, with changing drinking habits and the rise of craft beer establishments. Yet, the resilience of traditional pubs remains strong, with many adapting to modern trends while holding onto their historical roots. The pub continues to serve as a space for connection, where conversations can flourish, and friendships can blossom.

As I immersed myself in the British pub culture, I found a profound sense of connection to the history and tradition that surrounded me. The stories shared over pints of beer echoed the ongoing narrative of community and resilience, reminding me that, like the pubs themselves, we all have the capacity to create bonds that withstand the test of time.

Leaving the pub that night, I felt invigorated by the energy of the space and the connections I had made. It was a celebration of life—a reminder that even in a fast-paced world, there are still places where one can slow down, share a drink, and connect with others. In that spirit, I continued my exploration of Europe's drinking culture, eager to uncover the next chapter of my journey.

Part II: Personal Struggles and Reflections

Chapter 4: The Dance with Addiction

As I immersed myself in the rich tapestry of drinking culture across Europe, I couldn't help but reflect on my own relationship with alcohol. What began as a fascination with the rituals of drinking slowly morphed into something more insidious. The experiences that once brought me joy began to carry a weight I could no longer ignore.

Recognizing a Problem

In the early days of my travels, I enjoyed wine tastings in France, beer festivals in Germany, and cozy nights in British pubs without a second thought. I reveled in the beauty of each experience, believing I was merely participating in the cultural norm. But as time passed, a nagging feeling began to creep in—the sense that my drinking was no longer just a social activity.

Late nights turned into early mornings filled with regret. The fine line between enjoyment and dependence blurred, and I found myself drinking not just to celebrate but to escape the pressures and anxieties of life. As I settled into this pattern, the realization struck me: I was developing a dependency on alcohol that was starting to overshadow my experiences.

It was during one of my solo trips to a quaint seaside town in Portugal that the full weight of my dependency hit me. I had planned to enjoy a relaxing day exploring the coastline, but instead, I found myself sitting alone in a bar, nursing drink after drink. What was supposed to be a day of discovery transformed into an afternoon spent drowning my thoughts in a glass. In that moment, I felt a profound sense of sadness and isolation wash over me, illuminating the stark reality of my situation.

Cultural Pressures

The cultural acceptance of drinking across Europe complicated my struggle with alcohol. In many circles, drinking was synonymous with enjoyment, relaxation, and social bonding. The very traditions that celebrated community and connection began to feel like a trap. Each time I raised a glass, I felt the pressure to conform to the expectations of those around me.

In Germany, where beer is a staple at every gathering, I struggled to say no when offered a round by friends. In the pubs of London, I felt the weight of social expectations to keep pace with my companions, fearing judgment if I chose to abstain. These cultural norms masked my growing dependency, making it easy to rationalize my choices as part of the experience.

As I navigated these social situations, I often found myself grappling with guilt and shame. I wanted to enjoy the moment, yet I was becoming increasingly aware of the toll my drinking was taking on my health and relationships. I felt caught in a dance between societal acceptance and personal awareness, unsure of how to break free from the rhythm that was pulling me down.

Turning Point

The turning point came on a seemingly ordinary night in a bustling bar in Dublin. I had spent the evening enjoying the lively atmosphere, surrounded by laughter and music. As the night wore on, I lost track of time and the number of drinks I had consumed. At some point, I stepped outside for fresh air, feeling a wave of dizziness wash over me. The vibrant city lights blurred, and I stumbled on the pavement, catching myself just before falling.

In that moment of vulnerability, something shifted within me. I could no longer deny the reality of my drinking habits. I was overwhelmed by a sense of fear and clarity, realizing that I was spiraling. This was not just a harmless indulgence; it was a dangerous dance with addiction that threatened to take over my life.

I stood there in the cool night air, tears streaming down my face as I confronted the truth. I felt ashamed and frightened, but I also felt a flicker of resolve. I could no longer allow my fascination with European drinking culture to mask the damage I was inflicting on myself. It was time to take action.

As I made my way back inside, I knew that I needed to make a change. I decided to reach out for help, recognizing that this journey was about more than just enjoying the cultural experiences of Europe. It was about finding balance, understanding my relationship with alcohol, and reclaiming my life from the clutches of addiction.

That night marked a pivotal moment in my journey, one that would set the stage for deeper reflection and transformation. I was ready to confront my demons, ready to seek the support I needed to navigate the complexities of drinking culture while prioritizing my health and well-being. The dance with addiction was far from over, but I had taken the first step toward reclaiming my life.

Chapter 5: Seeking Help in a Drinking Culture

In the aftermath of my turning point in Dublin, I knew I needed to take decisive action to confront my relationship with alcohol. As I began to explore recovery options, I quickly discovered the complexities of seeking help in a culture where drinking is not only normalized but celebrated.

Exploring Recovery Options

My first step was to research various recovery programs available in Europe. I delved into literature about Alcoholics Anonymous, SMART Recovery, and other local support groups, trying to understand their approaches and philosophies. Each program offered a unique perspective on recovery, but I felt a particular pull towards the community aspect of A.A., where shared experiences could foster connection and healing.

I also learned about treatment centers that catered specifically to the needs of individuals struggling with alcohol dependency. While many of these centers were highly regarded, I hesitated at the thought of entering a residential program. The idea of withdrawing from daily life felt overwhelming, and I wasn't sure I was ready for such a significant commitment.

Instead, I sought out local A.A. meetings, hoping to find a supportive community that resonated with my experiences. I was curious to see how recovery was approached in different countries, particularly in light of their unique drinking cultures. The challenge, however, lay in breaking through the barriers that often made seeking help difficult.

Cultural Barriers

The normalization of drinking in European society presented a significant obstacle in my quest for recovery. In many social circles, alcohol is woven into the very fabric of life, making it challenging to navigate relationships while attempting to abstain. I could sense the discomfort that arose when I mentioned my desire to cut back on drinking. Friends often dismissed my concerns with well-meaning comments like, "You're fine, just enjoy yourself!" or "We all drink a bit too much sometimes; it's no big deal!"

This casual dismissal of my struggles highlighted a broader cultural barrier that many face when seeking help for addiction. In a society where drinking is often regarded as a rite of passage, admitting that one has a problem can feel like a betrayal of cultural norms. The fear of judgment loomed large, making it difficult to openly discuss my challenges without facing the stigma attached to addiction.

Moreover, the expectation to socialize over drinks often created situations that were fraught with temptation. Invitations to gatherings and events filled my calendar, and I found myself navigating a minefield of expectations. Each time I declined a drink, I felt the weight of scrutiny, and I worried about the implications of my choice. Would I be seen as a buzzkill or an outsider? The pressure to conform weighed heavily on me.

Support Systems

Amid these challenges, I began to understand the importance of support systems in navigating my recovery. I attended my first A.A. meeting in London, and as I entered the room filled with people sharing their stories, I felt an immediate sense of belonging. Here were individuals from diverse backgrounds, each with their own battles and triumphs. Their openness about their struggles mirrored my own, and for the first time, I felt understood.

The discussions that ensued were raw and honest, highlighting the commonality of our experiences. Hearing others talk about their cultural struggles with alcohol and the societal pressures they faced resonated deeply with me. In this space, I found solace and strength, realizing that I was not alone in my journey.

In addition to A.A., I sought support from friends who understood my commitment to sobriety. I reached out to Roy, my friend from Germany, and shared my challenges. His encouragement and insights provided me with reassurance and motivation. Having a support network of people who were genuinely invested in my recovery made a significant difference in my outlook.

I also began to explore online forums and resources, connecting with individuals in recovery from various European countries. These virtual communities offered valuable insights and strategies for coping with the pressures of social drinking. I learned about different cultural perspectives on sobriety and how others navigated the complexities of drinking culture.

Through these experiences, I discovered that seeking help in a drinking culture is not just about the programs and resources available; it's about cultivating a sense of community and connection. Support systems became the lifeblood of my recovery, reminding me that I didn't have to face this journey alone. Together, we could share our struggles, celebrate our victories, and forge a path toward healing.

As I immersed myself in recovery options and built a network of support, I felt a renewed sense of hope. I was beginning to understand that while the road ahead would be challenging, it was also filled with opportunities for growth and connection. I was ready to embrace the journey, armed with the knowledge that I could reclaim my life and rewrite my story, one step at a time.

Part III: A Journey Toward Healing

Chapter 6: Redefining Relationships

As I embarked on my path toward recovery, one of the most significant challenges I faced was the task of redefining my relationships. My drinking had strained connections with family and friends, leaving behind a trail of hurt and disappointment. I realized that healing wasn't just about my relationship with alcohol; it was also about mending the bonds that had been frayed by my past behavior.

Rebuilding Connections

I knew that the first step in rebuilding these connections was to approach them with honesty and vulnerability. My family, in particular, had endured my erratic behavior for too long. I decided to invite my parents over for dinner, a simple gesture that would allow us to reconnect in a meaningful way. As I prepared the meal, I felt a mix of anticipation and anxiety. Would they be able to forgive me? Would they understand the changes I was trying to make?

When they arrived, I greeted them with a warm hug, sensing the unspoken tension in the air. We sat down for dinner, and as we shared stories and laughter, I felt a flicker of hope. After the meal, I took a deep breath and opened up about my struggles with alcohol. I expressed my regrets for the pain I had caused and my commitment to sobriety.

To my relief, my parents listened with compassion. They shared their own feelings of worry and helplessness during my struggles, and in that moment, I felt the weight of our collective pain begin to lift. Through honesty, we began to rebuild the trust that had been fractured.

Newfound Clarity

As I continued my recovery journey, I discovered a newfound joy in socializing without the haze of alcohol. It was liberating to engage in gatherings with a clear mind, free from the fog of drunkenness. I found that conversations were richer, more meaningful. I could be present, truly listening to others, rather than lost in my thoughts or the effects of too many drinks.

One evening, I attended a friend's birthday party in London. As the festivities unfolded, I opted for sparkling water instead of beer. Initially, I felt a twinge of anxiety, worried about how others would perceive my choice. But as the night progressed, I found myself enjoying the conversations and laughter without the social lubricant of alcohol. I was fully engaged in the moment, connecting with friends in a way that felt genuine and fulfilling.

As I interacted with others, I realized that I could still be the life of the party, just without the crutch of alcohol. My friends appreciated my presence, and I was able to form deeper connections based on authenticity rather than superficiality. I felt empowered by my decision to embrace sobriety, and it became clear that my relationships could flourish in this new light.

Cultural Comparisons

Traveling through Europe, I began to notice cultural differences in how people approached socializing without alcohol. In Spain, for instance, gatherings often revolved around tapas and conversation, with many enjoying their meals without the pressure to drink. I attended a local festival where families came together to celebrate, and I marveled at how the focus was on food, laughter, and connection rather than alcohol. It was refreshing to see that joy could be found in community without the need for drinks.

Conversely, in the UK, I observed that while many embraced sobriety, the cultural expectation of drinking still lingered. At a pub in Edinburgh, I found myself surrounded by friends celebrating with pints, yet I felt comfortable sipping my non-alcoholic beverage. Some friends inquired about my choice, leading to open discussions about the pressures of drinking and the benefits of moderation. These moments of vulnerability fostered deeper connections and understanding among us.

Through these cultural comparisons, I gained insight into the diverse attitudes toward alcohol in different European contexts. Each country had its own customs and norms, but the common thread was the importance of connection—whether through shared meals, celebrations, or conversations. I realized that while the specifics of socializing might vary, the underlying desire for human connection remained universal.

In this chapter of my journey, I discovered the transformative power of redefining relationships. Through honesty, vulnerability, and a commitment to sobriety, I began to rebuild the connections that mattered most. The clarity I gained from socializing without alcohol opened my eyes to the depth of relationships I had once taken for granted.

As I embraced this new way of engaging with others, I felt a sense of fulfillment that had long eluded me. I was learning that true connection transcended the need for alcohol, allowing me to forge bonds that were authentic and lasting. My journey toward healing was not just about overcoming addiction; it was about rediscovering the beauty of relationships and the richness of life in all its forms.

Chapter 7: Embracing a Sober Lifestyle

As I settled into my new life of sobriety, I felt an invigorating sense of freedom and possibility. The fog that had clouded my judgment for so long was lifting, revealing a world brimming with opportunities to explore, connect, and grow. I realized that embracing a sober lifestyle was not merely about abstaining from alcohol; it was about rediscovering who I was and finding joy in new passions.

Finding New Passions

With a clear mind and a renewed sense of purpose, I sought out hobbies and interests that I had neglected during my years of drinking. I had always enjoyed cooking, but I had often turned to takeout or quick meals when I was busy socializing over drinks. Now, I found myself drawn to the kitchen once again. I enrolled in a local cooking class, eager to learn how to create traditional dishes from various European cuisines.

In that class, I discovered the joy of experimenting with flavors and techniques, transforming simple ingredients into delightful meals. The experience was cathartic; I poured my creativity into each dish, savoring the process as much as the outcome. Cooking became a therapeutic outlet, a way to express myself and share my love for food with others.

I also rekindled my love for art. Inspired by my earlier experiences in France, I began taking painting classes at a nearby studio. The act of creating brought me immense joy and satisfaction. I found solace in the strokes of the brush, allowing my emotions to flow onto the canvas. The world of art opened up a new avenue for self-expression, enriching my life in ways I had never anticipated.

Cultural Engagement

As I embraced these new passions, I also felt compelled to engage with European culture in a fresh, meaningful way. With alcohol no longer clouding my experiences, I was eager to explore the nuances of different cultures, from the intricate flavors of regional cuisines to the vibrant traditions that define each country.

I started attending food festivals, wine and cheese tastings, and cultural events where I could immerse myself in the local heritage. One particular event that stood out was a culinary festival in Bologna, Italy, where chefs showcased traditional recipes and cooking techniques. I wandered from stall to stall, savoring the rich flavors of handmade pasta and local cheeses, fully present in each moment. Without the influence of alcohol, I found myself appreciating the artistry behind each dish and the passion of the people who created them.

In Spain, I participated in a flamenco dance workshop. The rhythmic clapping of hands and the lively music filled the room with energy. I was nervous at first, but as I immersed myself in the dance, I felt a rush of joy. The experience reminded me that cultural engagement could be just as exhilarating and fulfilling as any social gathering centered around alcohol.

Personal Growth

Reflecting on my journey through sobriety, I recognized the profound changes in my perception of myself and my relationships. I had shed the layers of insecurity and self-doubt that had once defined me. Sobriety offered clarity, allowing me to understand my worth beyond the confines of alcohol.

I realized that I no longer needed to rely on drinks to connect with others. My relationships flourished as I engaged with friends and family on a deeper level. I could share my newfound passions with them, inviting them into my world of cooking, art, and cultural exploration. Together, we celebrated life in ways that were meaningful and fulfilling, without the need for alcohol to act as a social lubricant.

Moreover, I began to embrace vulnerability. I opened up about my struggles and triumphs, sharing my story with others who were also seeking change. My experiences became a source of inspiration, not just for me, but for those around me. I found strength in my vulnerability, realizing that it was a powerful catalyst for connection and understanding.

As I continued to embrace this sober lifestyle, I felt a profound sense of empowerment. I was no longer defined by my past; I was forging a new identity rooted in authenticity and resilience. The journey of recovery was not just about abstaining from alcohol; it was about reclaiming my life, discovering new passions, and engaging with the world in a way that was vibrant and full of possibility.

With each passing day, I became more confident in my choices and more grateful for the life I was building. I was excited to explore new experiences, deepen my connections, and continue growing as a person. Embracing a sober lifestyle had opened up a world of opportunities, and I was ready to dive in, fully present and alive.

Epilogue: A Toast to New Beginnings

As I sit here, pen in hand, I reflect on the remarkable journey I have undertaken—a journey that has transformed not only my relationship with alcohol but also my entire outlook on life. From the bustling streets of Paris to the beer gardens of Munich, I immersed myself in the vibrant drinking cultures of Europe, discovering the beauty and complexity of these traditions. Yet, amidst the revelry, I faced the stark reality of my own struggles with dependency, leading me to confront the role alcohol played in my life.

Through my experiences, I learned that alcohol is not just a drink; it is a lens through which we can examine our connections to culture, community, and ourselves. I came to understand that drinking can be both a celebration of life and a perilous dance with addiction. This duality forced me to confront the cultural pressures that glorify drinking while recognizing the importance of moderation and mindfulness in a world where alcohol is often woven into the very fabric of social interactions.

My transformation was not instantaneous; it was a gradual awakening that required vulnerability, honesty, and the willingness to seek help. With each step toward sobriety, I found new passions, forged deeper relationships, and engaged with the rich cultural experiences that life has to offer. I embraced a lifestyle free from the haze of alcohol, discovering joy in cooking, art, and the beauty of connection.

As I reflect on my journey, I feel a profound sense of gratitude—not just for the victories but also for the struggles that shaped me. I am reminded that every setback served as a lesson, and every moment of vulnerability strengthened my resolve. My experiences have equipped me with the understanding that recovery is not a destination but an ongoing process of growth and self-discovery.

To those who may be grappling with similar issues, I urge you to seek help. You are not alone in your struggles, and there is a community waiting to embrace you. Life beyond alcohol is not only possible; it can be a vibrant, fulfilling existence filled with joy and connection. There is no shame in seeking support, whether through friends, family, or recovery programs. Taking that first step can lead you down a path of empowerment and transformation.

In closing, I want to extend a hopeful message: it is possible to find joy in connection, culture, and community without the need for alcohol. Embrace the beauty of shared experiences, whether through a heartfelt conversation over coffee, a leisurely dinner with friends, or the thrill of exploring new passions. Life offers countless opportunities for connection, and each moment is a chance to celebrate without the crutch of alcohol.

So here's to new beginnings—to the friendships forged, the experiences cherished, and the love shared. Let us raise a toast to the journeys we embark upon, the lessons we learn, and the hope that guides us forward. The world is full of possibility, and it is ours to explore, one sober step at a time. Cheers!